ROBERT E. PEARY
AND THE
FIGHT
FOR THE
NORTH POLE

ROBERT E. PEARY
AND THE
FIGHT
FOR THE
NORTH POLE

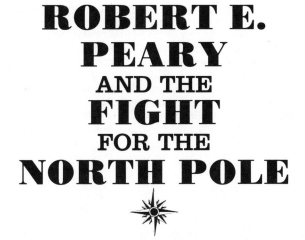

by Madelyn Klein Anderson

FRANKLIN WATTS
NEW YORK • LONDON • SYDNEY • TORONTO

Library of Congress Cataloging-in-Publication Data

Anderson, Madelyn Klein.
Robert E. Peary and the fight for the North Pole / by Madelyn Klein Anderson.
p.   cm.
Includes bibliographical references and index.
Summary: Examines the life of the explorer and his successful expedition to find the North Pole.
ISBN 0-531-15246-4 (trade).—ISBN 0-531-13004-5 (lib. bdg.)
1. Peary, Robert E. (Robert Edmund), 1856–1920—Juvenile literature. 2. Explorers—United States—Biography—Juvenile literature. 3. North Pole—Juvenile literature. [1. Peary, Robert E. (Robert Edmund), 1856–1920. 2. Explorers. 3. North Pole.]
I. Title.
G635.P4A63   1992
910'91632—DC20
[B]   91-33439   CIP   AC

CONTENTS

Prologue
11

CHAPTER I
Golden Days of Youth
13

CHAPTER II
Finding a Place in the World
23

CHAPTER III
In Sickness and in Health
37

CHAPTER IV
The Snow Baby
53

CHAPTER V
Matters of Living and Dying
69

CHAPTER VI
Great Explorations, Unmet Expectations
85

CHAPTER VII
The Brass Ring
95

CHAPTER VIII
In Victory—Agony
117

Epilogue
131

Source Notes
135

Bibliography
137

Index
139

ACKNOWLEDGMENTS

I am deeply grateful to Dr. Gerald F. Bigelow of the
Peary-MacMillan Arctic Museum and Arctic Studies Center and David R. Owen of Brooklyn College
of the City University of New York for their help.

ALSO BY
MADELYN KLEIN ANDERSON
ARTHRITIS
ENVIRONMENTAL DISEASES
OIL SPILLS

AUTHOR'S NOTE

"Eskimo" is a name derived from the French "Es-quimaux," a sixteenth-century Canadian priest's approximation of the Algonquian name for the people to their north, "Ush-ke-um-wau," which translates as "raw meat eaters." Over the past two decades, a political movement has evolved that uses an indigenous name instead of Eskimo. The name chosen was "Inuit," "the People," in Inuktitut.

Inuktitut is not the language spoken in Greenland, whose people figure in this book. In their language, they are "Talâdlit," which also means "the People." (Greenland is officially Talâdlit-Nunât, or "Land of the People.") In English and other languages, they refer to themselves as Eskimos or Greenlanders. (Many are of mixed black or white heritage after centuries of visitation and settlement by sailors, whalers, explorers, missionaries, and Danish government officials.)

In view of their own predilection and to be historically correct, the name "Eskimo" is used throughout this book. It is a name that can only inspire awe for a people of great bravery, fortitude, and generosity. That their role in polar exploration has been neglected in the history books is deplorable, and the author hopes in particular that one day the Eskimos Egingwah, Ooqueah, Seegloo, and Ootah will receive proper recognition along with Peary and Henson as co-discoverers of the North Pole.

A note, too, about the photographs that illustrate this book: Mostly taken around the turn-of-the-century in below-freezing temperatures by men wearing bulky mittens they dared not remove, the photographs often lack the clarity we are accustomed to today. It is hoped that their historic significance—their sheer wonder—compensates for any technical deficiency.

PROLOGUE

THE UNITED STATES CONGRESS, COMMITTEE OF NAVAL AFFAIRS SUBCOMMITTEE NUMBER EIGHT
Sat. Jan. 7
Tues. Jan. 10
Wed. Jan. 11, 1911
The committee having under consideration a bill for the purpose of promoting Captain Robert E. Peary to rear admiral for the discovery of the North Pole, which . . . would be to place in his hands . . . a passport into every phase of human society as an American hero and remembering that this country and every other country have been infested with bogus heroes as well as real ones . . . I want to find out whether your services to the Government have been of such moment as to make you worthy.[1]

He had gone forth and done battle with the Far North and had come home with a prize of mythic proportions to lay at the feet of his countrymen. He had expected honors, acclaim, and respect. Instead, he had been derided and reviled. Truly, *Tornarsuk* the devil was toying with him. Another man had claimed the prize of his hunt, and people had chosen to believe the falsehood. Now he had come to the most powerful men in his nation, demanding recognition, demanding vindication.

He had left his loved ones, endured such hardships as few had ever known, faced danger and death dozens of times over, suffered mutilation. He had not been defeated. But these few men could defeat him if they chose. They would decide whether his life had been spent in vain, his dreams valueless, and the sacrifices he had asked of himself and his loved ones pointless. No raging Arctic blizzard, no howling winds or deadly slivers of blowing ice, had caused him such agony as he was suffering now. Nothing in his life had prepared him for this. . . .

C H A P T E R

GOLDEN DAYS
OF
YOUTH

The practice of medicine was a hit-and-miss affair in the days before the Civil War. It was a trade practiced by old women healers who had gained their knowledge by nursing family and neighbors over the years; by peddlers of patent medicines; and by barbers, who kept their basins and razors handy in case they were asked to cut a sick person's vein to let out the "bad" blood—a favored cure for virtually every ailment.

But when Charles Nutter Peary fell sick, he wanted a real doctor. Who would take care of his wife and baby if he didn't get better soon? And, dear God, what if he were to die? He wanted to live. Mary and little Bertie needed him. So Peary undertook the arduous journey from his home in Washington Township (later to be called Cresson), Pennsylvania, to Pittsburgh, nearly eighty miles to the west, to get the help of a real doctor, although he would

13

have been as well served by the barber, the peddler, or the old women. The doctor's prescription—two teaspoons of cherry balsam and an "inhaling fluid" every three hours, a hot footbath, and a nightly bath with salt, brandy, and lemon juice—did not help. Charles Nutter Peary, husband and father, died of pneumonia in January 1859.

His young widow, frail all her life, but particularly so after the birth of her son, showed surprising strength in the matter of her future. Her husband's brothers wanted Mary and Bertie to stay on where they could watch after them and where the family business of making staves for barrels would support them, but Mary Wiley Peary had other ideas. She and Charles had come to Pennsylvania as newlyweds from their home in Maine. That was where Mary's father and the rest of her family lived, and it was where Charles's parents lived, and back to Maine she would go. She took her widow's share of the business, $12,000—a considerable sum in those days when a comfortable yearly salary might be $600—and settled in Cape Elizabeth. The town was near the city of Portland but far enough from family members living in Fryeburg to allow her to be independent. The money would allow Mary and her son to live decently, if not luxuriously, and Bertie would be able to go to school without ever having to work, the usual fate of a fatherless child.

Mary Peary was a loving mother, if somewhat overwhelmed by the son she had given birth to on that sixth day of May 1856. Robert, who was called Bertie, was a handful—an active child who, as he grew, seemed to delight in getting into all the mischief he could find. Some mischief found him, as when Mary put a bonnet on the young boy to protect his fair skin from the sun's rays. When Bertie's skin was constantly black-and-blue in the region of his blue eyes instead, his mother was bewildered. But rather than disobey his mother in the matter of the sunbonnet, Bertie chose to fight. There is no documentation of when the wearing of a bonnet stopped, but it could not have been long before even Mary Peary understood that a sunburn and freckles were better than an endless succession of black eyes, skinned elbows and knees, and torn clothes. Perhaps a word from one of Bertie's grandparents did the trick.

Bertie was only nine when the War between the States ended, and its effect on him must have been slight. Portland, however, was a departure point for troops and supplies, and activities among the staunch abolitionist Yankees from Maine must have had some impact on him. There undoubtedly was some correspondence from his uncles in Cresson, who might have found their barrel business improved by war or who may have written about the skirmishes that were common on the Pennsylvania–West Virginia state line. Fund-raising and bandage-rolling would have been regular activities in the houses of worship Bertie and his mother attended.

Bertie's mother did not fix on any one Protestant church group, but took him to one church or another every Sunday. Bertie also attended Sunday school regularly, and it was there that he first heard the siren call of the Arctic—at the tender age of six. A newspaper for children, the *Sunday School Advocate*, ran an article about Greenland, Eskimo children, and the explorations of Dr. Elisha Kent Kane. Only a few years before (1850–55), Dr. Kane and the men under him had established a new farthest-north record—the highest latitude reached in Arctic exploration. Forced to abandon their ship when it was trapped in crushing ice, Kane and his party made a harrowing trip south to civilization at Upernavik in

Greenland. Dr. Kane's writings about his Arctic explorations were hugely popular and were printed and reprinted in many editions. Bertie was entranced by the story, and his mother clipped the article out of the paper for him to read and reread. Dated March 22, 1862, the article is still among his memorabilia.

Bertie certainly didn't become obsessed by a desire to conquer the Far North at this age, however. He was far more interested in mischief, which was healthy—but annoying—in a young boy. Sad to say, Bertie's idea of fun was to trip his Grandfather Wiley on an errant foot or some other projection! He also liked to tease girls, throw stones at windows to hear the glass break, and toss off a manly but sacrilegious "Good God" now and then. Once, without thinking, he did this at the dinner table in front of the visiting pastor, causing Bertie to slide under the table in shame.

When he was eight or so, Bertie was sent to boarding school. There was a series of them, in Gorham, Topsham, Bethel, and Bridgton, perhaps because Mary Peary was seeking better or cheaper schools. Often, but not always, she moved into rooms nearby. While Bertie was a loving, concerned child—and man—he separated from his mother easily. He also fit in easily. At the Gorham school, for instance, he accepted that the boys were sneaking pins onto his chair so he'd be stuck when he sat down. "I guess they won't after a while" was all the young boy wrote to his mother, and they did stop doing it. Only a week later Bertie wrote, "We have had splendid times snowballing the last two or three days. We have made two snow forts out on the field. . . . This afternoon we are going to bathe. We bathe in the schoolroom every fortnight." (A bath every two weeks was not unusual in those days, when water had to be heated in buckets on a wood stove and tubs filled and emptied by hand.) When Bertie was nine and newly arrived at the school in Topsham, he wrote to his mother, "I . . . intended to write before but have been putting it off for I have had such good times playing with the boys in the gymnasium and out on the baseball ground."[1]

Bertie enjoyed being part of the group, but he also liked to spend time by himself, a trait he was to exhibit all his life. He took long walks, searching for places that looked interesting or particularly beautiful, where he could sit and look at the world around him and think. He would describe his observations to his mother in his letters, perhaps hoping also to capture them for himself.

Mary Peary bought a house in Portland when Bertie was ready for high school. For some reason, however, he didn't enter Portland High School until March 1870, near the end of the school year. But Bert made up all the work for the year and did it so well that his grade point average was 3.97 out of a perfect 4.0.

During that summer of 1870 Bert fell ill with something the family called "slow fever." This was probably typhoid, which makes a patient seem slow and dull. Recovery was also slow and dull. The time seemed to stretch out endlessly, and Bert amused himself as well as he could with books. He also began keeping a diary to develop his thinking—the beginning of a lifetime habit. Not until January 1871 was Bertie able to get around freely. His doctors recommended lots of sunshine and fresh air, a little difficult to get during January in Maine, so two of Bertie's relatives took him south to the Carolinas and Georgia. He enjoyed himself there tremendously, exploring, collecting rock specimens, perfecting his bird-watching skills, and recording everything in his diary. He made a number of friends and was well liked even though he was a Yankee and—almost as bad—still fond of teasing girls.

By April Bert was able to go back to school, and once again he made up all the work by June. Having to catch up on schoolwork two years in succession didn't give him much time to have fun. Bert made up for that in his junior and senior years, when the pace of a full school year must have seemed leisurely indeed. His circle of friends expanded rapidly, he was a leader in school activities, and girls suddenly ceased to be objects to tease and trick. One girl, known only as Em, began showing up in his diary with increasing frequency.

Bert was at his happiest when sailing or tramping in the woods, alone or with two or three friends. His love of birds and his skill at observing them developed into an expertise of such proportions that, although he was still in high school, he was invited to lecture on the subject at the Portland Museum of Natural History. Bert also taught himself the craft of taxidermy, preserving and displaying birds and small animals for study and for the enjoyment of having them in his room. Some he found dead in the woods, and some he shot. (This was not frowned upon in his day. No one even gave it a second thought.)

Nature was not Bert's only passion. He was also a constant patron of the public library, and he attended every cultural activity Portland had to offer. He enjoyed writing and was ecstatic when an essay he wrote on Adam and Eve was published in the school newspaper. He took up the much admired art of declamation—public speaking—although he had to work hard to overcome a slight lisp. And then there were the young ladies. On January 16, 1873, when Bert was sixteen and a half, he confided to his diary some thoughts on that subject: "I have bought tickets to Mrs. Dickenson's lecture tonight. . . . At last [Em] yielded to my persuasions and got ready. It was very slippery. Consequently she clung to me closer than usual which, of course, was pleasant to me. . . . Going home it was more slippery than ever, which was good for me." A few weeks later, on February 16, 1873, he wrote that Em "thought sliding was splendid . . . and said she was sorry she had never tried it before . . . and in this way we passed the time until 10:30. We went home . . . [and] I asked for a kiss. Of course, she refused but it was not a very decided one, and I am going to take one some evening."[2] And he did.

A few months later, in June 1873, Bert graduated from high school and was one of the honored student speakers. His topic was Nature's Mysteries, one of which was what man would find should he ever reach the North Pole.

Bert applied for and won a tuition scholarship to nearby Bowdoin College. He sold his beloved collection of stuffed birds for book money. Mary Peary gave up her house and took rooms near the college, about twenty-five miles from Portland. Perhaps she could not afford to give Bert money for his own place, or perhaps she knew that once he graduated from college, it would not be long before he would be gone from her forever. For whatever reason, and again despite attempts by relatives to dissuade her, off she went with Bert to college.

Bert really didn't mind. They moved into rooms on the second floor of a boardinghouse on Lincoln Street in Brunswick, Maine, which Bert described in his diary as "the prettiest street I ever saw." He didn't think much of the town otherwise; it seemed too provincial, too dull, after city life in Portland.

And he was homesick for his friends. The country-
side was inviting, however, and he went on long
rambles and started a new bird collection. As a
freshman, he was put in charge of the class pro-
gram for the school's annual Ivy Day and was
elected to serve as archivist for the celebration. The
following year he was chosen to compete in the
sophomore declamation contest. By then he had
largely overcome his lisp, and public speaking had
reinforced his determination to succeed despite a
seeming handicap. Bert enjoyed the competition,
but he preferred to compete individually rather than
as part of a team. He didn't want to be a loser because of the failure of others. He sculled for one
winning season, but when he felt the team couldn't
do it again, he didn't go out for the next season. He
hiked, he sailed, he bobsledded, and he even won a
baseball-throwing contest.

Not until Bert's junior year, however, did things
come together for him at Bowdoin. A professor,
George Leonard Vose, fired up Bert's enthusiasm.
Vose was a teacher who spoke to the point, who cut
through verbiage and demanded solid perfor-
mances from his pupils. His subject was civil
engineering—the planning, building, and mainte-
nance of public works such as bridges, canals,
piers, and roads. Vose's many years of experience,
his practical approach to teaching, and his close-
ness to his students was just what Bert needed. And
Bert was the kind of student who could inspire such
a professor. Bert worked for days on a problem everyone else had given up on, and he finally found a
solution. Vose was amazed, declaring it the best
piece of work ever done in the school's civil engineering department. That left no doubt in Bert's
mind: he would be a civil engineer.

Bert often worked from five in the morning to

eight or nine at night on his projects, but he didn't neglect his burgeoning social life. He was elected to Phi Beta Kappa for scholastic achievement, and he was elected to a social fraternity as well, Delta Kappa Epsilon.

In one of his letters at this time, he wrote, "I should like to gain that attractive personality that when I was with a person they should always have to like me, whether they wanted to or not."[3]

Tall and athletic, sporting a mustache now, Bert was making the acquaintance of most of the eligible young ladies in the area. But there was a girl in Portland—Mary Kilby, called Mae, and probably the Em of his high school days—whom he favored. He visited her often, walking the twenty-five miles to Portland and then back the next day.

In the summer of 1876, Bert walked to Portland and then took a packet boat to New York City and a train to the Centennial Exposition in Philadelphia. The exposition fired his imagination and his pride in his country and its people. He was enthusiastic about the promise of the future and wanted to be an important part of it, to do something special.

Soon the future became the present, and graduation day for the class of 1877 was upon him. Bert ranked second in his class, having made a conscious decision not to go for first place because he would have had to give up too much enjoyment in the effort. He did write the class ode; unfortunately, his poetry was as prosaic as his prose was poetic.

Like most other graduates, Bert left his alma mater with regret and with some trepidation. What lay ahead? Bert had no idea, but he knew he would not settle for dullness or mediocrity. He would have been joyous had he known then that he would become one of the most illustrious graduates of Bowdoin College.

C H A P T E R

FINDING
A PLACE
IN THE
WORLD

Robert E. Peary, brand-new civil engineer, was aware of the fact that Fryeburg, Maine, was not the place to practice his hard-won skills. But his mother bought a new house there to be near her family, and Bert went with her. Why Bert didn't get tapped for a job and why he didn't strike out for Portland is not known. Perhaps there were few openings at the time, or perhaps he was tired after all that work and play at Bowdoin and needed time to think.

In Fryeburg he cultivated new friends and acquaintances and earned money with his taxidermy. His work was highly skilled and brought him more and more customers and a certain amount of local fame. So did his horsemanship, particularly his ability to break in horses. His reputation stood him in good stead, and in 1878 he was appointed a justice of the peace for Oxford County. He seems to have had plenty of time left over for other things such as camping, collecting botanical samples for classification and study, and studying German and mathematics. He also wrote a lot of letters to Mary Kilby, and soon they were engaged to be married.

Mary stayed in Portland, however, and Bert in Fryeburg, except for a few carefully chaperoned exchange visits. What Mary did in Portland during the period of her engagement to Bert is not known, but in Fryeburg, Bert kept up his social life with the local young women. He also sharpened his civil engineering skills and mapped the entire village. He walked off distances and calculated elevations and did all the other things that go into making a good map, spending weeks on the drawing. All this was meant to be for his satisfaction alone, but it soon proved more meaningful.

A poster at the Fryeburg post office announced that the U.S. Coast and Geodetic Survey was accepting applications for trial appointments as draftsmen. Bert applied, and to demonstrate his skill, he sent his map of Fryeburg along with the required papers. To his joy, he was accepted. He left Fryeburg on July 4 for Portland, where he said good-bye to Mary and took a packet boat to New York and then a train to Washington, D.C.

When Bert reported for work, he discovered, to his pleasure, that one of the other appointees was a classmate from Bowdoin, Al Burton. The two decided to room together and found lodgings in a boardinghouse not far from their office. Their salary was ten dollars a week, and they worked from nine to four on Monday through Friday and nine to three on Saturday. Staff members were not allowed to leave the building even for the hour lunch break, and for the first time Bert became an indoor person. While the job was new, Bert didn't mind so much. All his job consisted of, however, was practicing lettering, to prepare for annotating charts and maps and writing reports. The work was dull. In November Bert wrote to his mother, "These moments of irresistible longing for the freedom of the open air do not come to me quite as often as usual, but they come with increasing force every time, and some day they will get away with me and I shall wreck the traces."[1] He didn't, but he dreamed.

Bert did break his engagement to Mary Kilby, a commitment he had regretted almost as soon as he entered into it. He could not see himself working at a tedious job all his life in order to support a wife and family; he wanted to be free to find fame and fortune. A bit reluctantly, Mary Kilby gave a relieved Bert his freedom.

Only two weeks later, in January 1880, the Coast and Geodetic Survey gave him a permanent appointment. Bert was jubilant, not because a permanent job doing something he didn't like suddenly became more exciting—if anything, it was rather appalling to him—but because he had succeeded, and succeeded well: he had topped the list of appointees. Knowing he would be staying in Washington led him to broaden his activities to escape some of the boredom of his days. He joined a club with a swimming pool, and he took dancing lessons, which was important in those days for a young man who wanted an entry into society.

Bert also read avidly and spent a lot of time reading about a proposed canal in Central America that would connect the Atlantic and Pacific oceans. This would be a venture worthy of a young civil engineer seeking fame. But even as he dreamed of exotic places and deeds, he used his savings to buy an island, Eagle Island, off the coast of Maine, a place he had loved as a boy. He did so to ensure that he would have roots somewhere in the world, and the island did not disappoint him; it was his sanctuary until he died.

Seeking excitement, Bert thought about working in Central America and wrote to his mother to ask for her blessing. He hoped she would understand his deep needs and give her consent to his going so far away. "I feel myself overmastered by a restless desire to do something. . . . There are men who are capable of becoming machines and there are men who can do nothing unless permitted to do it [on] their own, and the world has need of both. If it was a case of daily bread with me, it would be different, but I do not strive for money, but for fame, though money as a secondary consideration would be no objection."[2] Bert's mother ignored his plea. She loved this only child of hers and would have given him almost anything, but this dangerous work she could not condone. Bert faced down her silence, urgently requesting an answer. It came, but it was not the one he wanted. His mother said no, and Bert bowed to her wishes.

But not for long. How could it be for long when his need was so strong? He wrote in his diary,

> Columbus, Cortez, Livingstone . . . Balboa, DeSoto, and all the host of travelers and explorers . . . sometimes I can feel something of the thrill and blended aroma of all such first views since the world was in its infancy. . . . I have stood upon the summit of a mountain . . . have given my imagination full sway, until I know I have felt something of that same thrill that Cortez felt when . . . he gained the summit of the last range of mountains that lay between him and the city of the Aztecs. . . . And as for Balboa, one moment such as that when, bidding his followers halt, alone he climbed the last rock upon that "peak in Darien," and saw beyond the tree tops the flashing waves of

that great mysterious ocean, was worth years of ordinary life. . . . I am glad that my lot is cast upon the world now rather than later when there will be no new places.[3]

Over a year would go by before his longing for far-off places would become reality. Bert watched and waited for an opportunity. Then, as so often happens, two knocked on his door at the same time. One was an offer of a draftsman's job in Mexico; the other was a chance to take the examination for an appointment as a civil engineer with the United States Navy. Bert decided to try for one of the naval appointments, and again he appended examples of his drawings to support his application. About two months later he opened the newspaper one day to find on a list of new naval appointees: "Robert E. Peary, Lieutenant, U.S.N." Bert resigned immediately from the U.S. Coast and Geodetic Survey, bought naval uniforms, and went home to Maine to celebrate.

Navy pay was good and eased his life considerably. His security was ensured, and adventure beckoned. So did the Washington social scene. Bert was young, tall, presentable—some might even say handsome—and he wore his uniform well. The dancing lessons he had taken came in handy, and he was often seen at Marini's, a popular dance place. Among the many young ladies he met there was Josephine Diebitsch, the daughter of a Smithsonian Institution scholar. Josephine was of particular interest to him, but that would have to wait.

The new Lieutenant Peary was not completely unknown to the Navy. His interest in a Central American canal had come to their attention, possibly during their investigation of his suitability as an officer. Bert was immediately claimed as an assistant to A. G. Menocal, a civil engineer assessing the feasibility of a canal across Nicaragua.

Nicaragua was not to be Lieutenant Peary's first assignment, however. Instead, he was sent to the naval supply depot at Key West, Florida, to keep an eye on the building of a pier by a civilian company. Peary prepared for the assignment by studying everything he could find on the project and the terrain. This thorough preparation was a practice he followed all his life. But when he got to Key West, no one would listen to the ideas of a young engineer and lieutenant. The civilian contractor was antagonistic, and so was the commanding officer, who was a U.S. Naval Academy graduate. Peary had his first experience with an attitude that he would run into for the rest of his life: the disdain that Naval Academy graduates expressed for all other commissioned officers. Peary was an appointee whose official title was civil engineer and whose rank of lieutenant was meant only to place him on a particular pay-scale level. He was not "Navy."

Peary's cup of misery overflowed when he came down with yellow fever, a dangerous and endemic disease in that climate in those days. Hot with fever and in pain, he was bedded down for two weeks. When he got back to his job, he found things in a mess. Work had stopped because underwater debris was preventing the laying of the foundations for the pier. Peary rigged a torpedo and blasted a small area free, but he was forbidden to blast further, on the ground that he was imperiling the workers. The men were already demoralized by their fear of contracting yellow fever, and it seemed that the job might go on forever. Peary was within the bounds of his authority to order all work stopped, and he did so, rather a brave act for a new officer. He was recalled to Washington to give an explanation, which he did so well that he was sent back to Key

West with specific orders to build the pier his way. He blasted, and he designed new equipment, and three months later, in the spring of 1883, the pier was ready—at a savings of 10 percent of the funds allotted.

Peary returned to Washington in triumph, but there was no reward of another exciting assignment. Instead, there were many months of desk duty. Then, as 1884 drew to a close, the government signed a treaty with Nicaragua, and a canal became feasible. Menocal was in charge, and Peary was to work for him. By Christmas Day, Peary was sailing through the Caribbean Sea. As the ship passed San Salvador, he wrote his mother about this "birthplace of the New World, land which first gladdened the eyes of Columbus, purple against the yellow sunset as it was nearly 400 years ago when it smiled a welcome to this man whose fame can be equaled only by him who shall one day stand with 360° of longitude beneath his motionless foot, and for whom East and West shall have vanished: the discoverer of the North Pole."[4]

Did Peary think of himself as that man at that time? Perhaps. He was headed in the opposite direction, but he was still daydreaming about the Far North.

Peary spent three months in 1885 exploring eastern Nicaragua's swamps and jungles, where "all the men and myself as well [were] constantly [in water] to our knees and waists and even necks, cutting, lifting, pulling, pushing, swimming." Peary was able to shorten the planned route by miles, offering a projected savings to the United States of $17 million. But the plans for a canal were put on the shelf, the idea temporarily stalled. Back to Washington he went. Again he was praised for a job well done, but again he was put behind a desk.

A good deal of free time allowed Peary to get

29

better acquainted with Josephine Diebitsch and also with the local bookstores. He came across a copy of *Exploration of Interior Greenland,* written in 1870 by the Swedish explorer Nils Adolf Erik Nordenskjöld. Baron Nordenskjöld had achieved fame, and his title, for the discovery in 1878–79 of the Northeast Passage through Arctic waters across the top of Europe to the Orient. Just as he had as a child, Peary succumbed to the romance of the Arctic and read everything he could find about it. There was quite a bit—books written by whalers, explorers in search of the Northwest Passage across North America to Asia, and members of rescue parties searching for lost explorers. The disappearance of Sir John Franklin and his men had triggered over forty search missions, among them the one led by Elisha Kent Kane, whose story had so entranced the six-year-old Bertie.

Peary undoubtedly had access also to information garnered from the International Polar Year (1882), in which eleven countries had started an in-depth study of the Arctic. The United States had set up one station, on Ellesmere Island, under the command of an inexperienced young Army lieutenant, Adolphus Greely, and then had neglected to support it. In 1885, when Peary was devouring information on the Arctic, there was a great stir in the newspapers after a rescue ship sent to Ellesmere Island returned with only eight of the twenty-six men in the Greely party. The others had died of exposure, starvation, and scurvy; one had committed suicide; and another had been executed for stealing supplies. Cannibalism had added to their terror.

Perhaps this failed effort impelled Peary to make minutely detailed notes on expedition tactics in his diary for 1885. Perhaps it was simply an intellectual exercise, or perhaps he had already decided to become an explorer of the Arctic. Whatever the reasons, Peary laid out a plan for Arctic travel that, in its broad outlines, he was to follow in all the years to come. He would use Greenland as a base. He would live as the Eskimos did, housing and clothing his men and himself in Eskimo fashion. Most explorers of the time rejected the idea of "turning native" as beneath them. Peary realized that this was pure prejudice. He believed that it was vital to draw upon the Eskimos' centuries of knowledge of how to survive in the Arctic.

Peary had his prejudices, too, of course, including the then common notion that whites were mentally and culturally superior to people of other races. This resulted in Peary's assuming what was commonly called "the white man's burden," a broad kind of paternalism. His plans called for white men as leaders or "heads" of the expedition body, while members of other races were its arms and legs. But he tempered this prejudice in ways that his more stiff-necked peers would have found shocking. It would be ideal, he thought, if white men took Eskimo wives so as to breed an Arctic race combining white intelligence with Eskimo physical strength. He never entertained the thought that it might not work quite that way.

And Peary's ideas about women were also quite advanced for his time: "In all expeditions where women have taken part they have been of as much or more assistance than the men . . . and I am not sure but what a party of which the larger properties were women would be best." But he also wrote, "It is asking too much of masculine human nature to expect it to remain in an Arctic climate enduring constant hardship, without one relieving feature. Feminine companionship not only causes greater contentment, but as a matter of both mental and physical health and the retention of the top notch of manhood it is a necessity."[5]

Peary studied what was known of the water currents and the ice patterns in the area and worked on plans for sledges and a system of shelters along the line of march. His basic food would be the kind that Indians used on long journeys—pemmican, dried and shredded meat and berries pressed into patties. Pemmican would not spoil, was not as heavy as other foods to carry, and would not require precious fuel for cooking. Peary would stay in the Arctic until the weather was favorable for an expedition, even if that meant waiting over a season or two. Peary worked all of this out without ever having spent a single day in the Arctic, and the plan was to prove serviceable many years later.

All this research and planning could lead to only one conclusion: Peary had to see this world of ice for himself. In May 1886 he took six months' leave, borrowed $500 from his disapproving but indulgent mother, and took off for Greenland. His ship put in first at Saint John's, Newfoundland, where he bought himself clothing and other supplies and a large sledge with a tobogganlike front end against which the supplies could be secured. Then he took passage on a whaler for Godhavn, the capital of the northern district of Greenland. Godhavn did not welcome Peary with open arms. To the contrary, the Danish government there wanted no part of young adventurers who longed to make a solitary trip across the inland ice, the vast ice cap covering most of Greenland. But Peary had not come so far to be turned away. He knew that asking permission to enter was more or less a courtesy. At the time, the United States did not recognize Danish sovereignty over anything but the inhabited parts of Greenland, and most people viewed the rest as international territory. But Peary was a naval officer and did not want any international incidents, so he exercised his charm and powers of persuasion and soon gained permission to enter.

From Godhavn, Peary went farther north by boat to a small settlement, Ritenbenk, that clung to the base of the mountains he would have to climb to reach the ice cap. Here he was lucky. He met a Danish young man, Christian Maigaard, who wanted to accompany him. The Eskimos would not go on the inland ice. To them it was taboo, the home of the dead. For Peary to have gone alone would have been extremely dangerous. He required the help of at least one other man in facing the crevasses (deep cracks in the snow and ice), the icy pools of summer meltwater, and the other dangers as yet unknown.

Climbing the mountains to reach the ice cap took the two men three days. When they finally reached the ice cap, they were engulfed in fog, sleet, snow, and winds of gale force—everything nature could throw at them. When this bombardment finally stopped, the men saw that a blizzard was brewing and prudently climbed back down the mountain to wait it out. The second climb was easier, since they were not encumbered by supplies, having left the bulk of them behind on the ice cap. Now they had to cross snow arches over the many crevasses that bordered the inland ice. Every step had to be tested, and only quick reflexes kept them from falling into the yawning pits on one or two occasions. Each man did fall into icy pools of water, but the other man was able to help him out and into dry clothing. The ice cap did not have as many traps once the outer rim was broached. A two-day gale that whipped the snow into a cutting frenzy, impenetrable fog, and the blinding glare of sunlight on the mirrorlike ice were lesser obstacles.

Using skis and dragging their sledges, Peary and Maigaard traveled about one hundred miles inland, breaking Baron Nordenskjöld's record by twenty-five miles or so to become the new record-holders. Then the two men turned back. They had only six days' worth of food left and would face starvation if bad weather delayed them. The wind was from the east, at their backs, on the return journey. This gave them the idea of lashing their sledges side by side and rigging a mast and sail to form a kind of catamaran. They made a rudder from a hatchet, held on to the mast, and let the wind move them lightly, steadily, and very, very quickly across the snow arches bridging the crevasses.

Soon the men were climbing down from the ice to the village. Here Peary met the ship that had brought him up and was to take him home. Christian Maigaard probably went back to Denmark with his interest in the inland ice satisfied, because there is no further mention of him in Arctic annals.

Peary, on the other hand, wanted more. The record for the inland ice brought him a certain amount of fame, and it was hard for Peary to return to the "commonplace drudgery" of his desk job with the navy. "I want my fame *now* while you too can enjoy it," he wrote to his mother, imploring her approval—and funds—for a second trip. She wrote back with words to the effect that he was aging her rapidly by exposing himself to such danger, and she warned, too, that "such fame [as you desire] is dearly bought." She was quite right, but Robert Peary would have it no other way.

There was to be a detour, however, in Peary's quest. In the spring of 1887, interest in the Nicaraguan canal was once again revived, this time by a private group, the Maritime Canal Company. Menocal became chief engineer for the company,

Peary his assistant. Both were still in the Navy, but this project was of interest to the government, which allowed them to assume a dual military and civilian role. The company paid Peary $400 a year and the navy paid him $6,200 and put him on leave. Peary's crew would consist of forty-five to fifty engineers, including Emil Diebitsch, Josephine's brother, and about one hundred laborers to be signed on in Jamaica and Nicaragua.

While preparing for his trip, Peary walked into a Washington store to buy a hat. He was waited on by a young black man whose manner impressed him. Peary always prided himself on his ability to make quick, accurate judgments about people, and he made one then. What was the young man's name? Would he be willing to become Peary's batman—an officer's personal attendant? The man's name was Matthew Henson, and he agreed to take on the job. Although carried on Peary's payroll as a manservant and referred to as such in most books and articles, Matt Henson seems to have acted in this capacity for only a very short time at the beginning of their relationship. From their first Nicaraguan venture, when Henson was made a chainman on a surveying gang, until they reached the North Pole, Henson was Peary's valued assistant, not his servant.

Peary was enthusiastic about this Nicaraguan venture. He was being freed from the thing he dreamed most—the day-to-day drudgery of a desk job. He would travel, he would have many men under his command, and a reporter from the *New York Herald* would accompany the survey and would publicize his work. Once again, Peary prepared thoroughly for his assignment. He dictated long memorandums on the work to be done, the food service, the sanitation facilities, the medical problems that might arise and how they might be avoided or treated, and the many other difficulties of daily living on a jungle expedition. Peary wrote to his engineers about the importance of keeping detailed records and told them, "You must be especially careful in your treatment of your Nicaraguan (and Jamaican) employees. While docile and willing to work almost without exception, they are not accustomed to profanity or personal chastisement or abuse, and you and the officers in your party will endeavor by a proper combination of firmness and kindness to control and direct them without recourse to either."[6] This kind of concern, this consideration and respect for the sensibilities of his crewmen—and later of the Eskimos—was characteristic of Peary. Yet in the future, this characteristic, this strong sense of responsibility, would be construed by some as autocratic, even dictatorial.

The 4,000-mile survey through extremely difficult and dangerous jungle terrain took seven months. But it was not all jungle and hardship. Keeping Nicaragua happy with the idea of a canal was also part of Peary's job. He went to Managua, the capital, for two meetings with Nicaragua's president and was a guest at a glittering state ball. The reporter from the *Herald* and another from the *New York Times* accompanied him, and Robert Peary's name, to his delight, was brought to the attention of the nation.

When the survey was over and Peary returned home, again there were no promotions, no exciting assignments, no rewards other than a "well done." But there *was* Josephine Diebitsch, and she married him.

C H A P T E R

III

IN SICKNESS
AND IN
HEALTH

Attractive, smart, robust, adventuresome, adapt-able, Josephine Diebitsch—called Jo—was the per-fect wife for Robert Peary, although he could only have guessed that on August 11, 1888, the day they were married. After a brief honeymoon at the sea-side in then-elegant Sea Bright, New Jersey, the newlyweds went to Bert's new posting in New York City.

Peary was stationed at the New York Naval Ship-yard, better known as the Brooklyn Navy Yard. The newlyweds never lived in Brooklyn, however, choosing instead to stay in Manhattan and take ad-vantage of the activities that borough offered. They rented rooms in a boardinghouse on Madison Ave-nue near the mansion of John Pierpont Morgan, then they moved a few blocks away to Fifth Avenue and Thirty-second Street, a short block from where the Empire State Building stands today. This was a long commute for Bert in those horse-and-buggy days, although the new Brooklyn Bridge made the daily trip between the two boroughs a lot easier.

The Pearys were a handsome couple, both tall, graceful, well dressed, and happy. They would walk for miles, striding up Fifth Avenue to Central Park—about the closest Bert could get to nature—or just wandering about town. Two months after their marriage, Jo wrote to Mary Peary that "if Bert is as happy as I am then we must be the happiest people in the world."

Bert was undeniably happy, but not so content. His ambitions had not changed, and he was getting restless to achieve them. Fridtjof Nansen had crossed Greenland's ice cap, a feat that Peary had wanted for himself, and Nansen was younger than he was. Nansen's book, *First Crossing of Greenland,* had mentioned Peary and his use of wind power to travel on the ice cap. Would Peary never be more than a footnote in the history of Arctic exploration?

In 1890 Bert was transferred to Philadelphia's League Island Navy Yard. He and Jo took rooms on fashionable Elm Avenue across from Fairmount Park. Bert went to his desk every day, and his dream of Arctic exploration began to fade. Alarmed, he made a conscious decision not to let that happen and began to try to turn the dream into reality. He knew that Jo would not try to hold him back from doing what he felt he must; that was one of the reasons he had married her. He wrote to various geographical societies and science organizations, seeking financial support for a crossing of the Greenland ice cap in the north. Was Greenland an island or a continent extending to the top of the world? Were there people living in some habitable section of the inland ice, as the Eskimos believed? The responses to Peary's letters were negative, but one organization, the Brooklyn Institute, asked if he would talk to its members about his Greenland trip—for a fee, of course. Peary said he would. He carefully prepared a presentation, practiced his speaking skills, and, dressed in his Arctic gear and dragging his sledge, he conquered the Brooklyn audience. He realized that if people in Brooklyn were interested enough to pay hard-earned cash to listen to him, audiences elsewhere would also want to hear him. He prepared for an extracurricular life on the lecture circuit, hoping to earn enough money to finance an expedition himself.

Then suddenly the wheel turned: instead of saying no, the Brooklyn Institute, the American Geographical Society, and the Philadelphia Academy of Natural Sciences all said yes, they would lend their support to an expedition. An ecstatic Peary chartered a ship, the *Kite*, and set to work. Scientists and others who wanted to go to Greenland asked to be taken along as paying passengers. Peary welcomed their financial contribution but was careful to explain that the money would not give them any voice in the management of the expedition. Command would be his alone; he wanted no dissension of any kind to destroy his mission, as it had so many others' endeavors. All parties agreed, at least in theory, and the First North Greenland Expedition was on its way to becoming reality.

Peary threw himself into preparations. He was convinced that a small party stood the best chance of success. Previous Arctic expeditions had been large and unwieldy, hard to provision and discipline. Fewer people did not need so much food and could live off the land if that became necessary, and the teamwork required would be easier to achieve. They would not pull sledges on this trip as he and Christian Maigaard had done; that was too tiring.

Instead, they would travel the Eskimo way, driving dog teams harnessed to sledges. Eskimo dogs could pull 100 pounds of supplies day after day for twenty to thirty days; with lesser amounts, they could cover a hundred or more miles in a single day's run on good surfaces. If supplies ran low, the weakest dogs could be slain and used as food. (Peary loved animals, but he was a realist about starvation.) The party would learn Eskimo hunting skills, and Eskimo women would make them clothing and tend to the needs of the men.

And Jo would be there for him. Bert was determined to show that the Arctic need not be the place of terror previous disastrous expeditions had made it seem, and that white women as well as Eskimo women could live in the high Arctic. Jo was equally determined not to be left behind. The world was shocked at this, and she had some problems with family and with writers of nasty letters, but that only fixed her determination. After all, this was 1891, and she was a modern woman!

Igloos—as all Eskimo houses were called, whether they were built of stone and sod, skins, or blocks of snow—were extremely small and offered no privacy. Therefore Bert designed a house that could be built by the members of the expedition from the packing cases and other lumber they would bring with them; wood was virtually nonexistent in those latitudes. They would also bring tea, sugar, spices, cans of food and milk, and wines; Bert planned for a year's stay. The ship could not take them north until summer temperatures had melted, or at least softened, the sea ice, usually in July. Then the clothing had to be prepared, and the novices to Arctic travel had to learn techniques of snowshoeing and skiing and dog- and sledge-handling. By then the long winter darkness would be on them, and they would not be able to travel until daylight returned, in late February. A party would cross the northern ice cap around April, while at the base camp the rest of the men and Jo would collect scientific data on tides, animals, rocks, the Eskimos, and so on. In the summer, when it was always daylight, the ship would return for them and they would finish their tasks and get out. Otherwise, fall's twilight and dropping temperatures would freeze them in for six or eight more months.

The expedition members would include Matthew Henson; Dr. Frederick A. Cook, a physician, and later Peary's nemesis, who would also act as ethnologist, collecting data on the Eskimos; Langdon Gibson, an ornithologist who would study the birds of Greenland and act as chief hunter; Elvind Astrup, a young Norwegian familiar with traveling on snow; and John Verhoeff, an American who paid the then princely sum of $2,000 to join the group and who would serve as expedition meteorologist, recording wind and weather conditions, and mineralogist, collecting rock specimens. Nine scientists from the Philadelphia Academy of Sciences went with the expedition as paying passengers for the ship's journey up and back.

Peary obtained a year's leave from the Navy at half pay, and the North Greenland Expedition was ready. On June 8, 1891, the *Kite* set forth from a pier in Brooklyn for Greenland. Peary had a deep, almost mystical, sense of purpose. From Sydney, Nova Scotia, he posted a letter to his mother that said in part, "now I feel that all is written in the irrevocable book, that I have been selected for this work and will be . . . carried safely and successfully through."[1]

On the leg of the journey from Nova Scotia to Greenland, the *Kite* encountered pack ice, floes of sea ice moving down from the Arctic Ocean on the tides and currents, and soon was stuck fast. Jo and the others clambered over the side, glad to stretch their legs and excited at the thought of taking a walk on the ocean. As the weather warmed a little, the *Kite* was able to break up the ice floes, "just as you would shiver a sheet of taffy when you strike it a sharp, hard blow," Jo wrote in her diary.

She was to discover, however, that the ice did not always break that easily. Jo and Bert enjoyed watching the ice-breaking process from the bridge of the ship, and Bert often went behind the wheel-house to watch as the ship backed up as a first step for charging the ice. One day the ship's rudder struck an ironlike mass of ice below the waterline. The ship's tiller, the bar that moved the rudder, caromed against Bert's leg, pinning him and moving inexorably until the bones in his leg snapped with a sickening crunch. Jo and the helmsmen rushed to the aid of the white-faced, agonized Bert, standing now on one leg and telling Jo not to be worried.

The two doctors aboard, Cook and D. R. Sharp of the Philadelphia Academy contingent, set Bert's leg in a boxlike contraption to keep the bones in place. For several days, only morphine eased the pain. Bert was fearful that without his guidance, the scientists aboard might want to abort the expedition. One of the academy members did, in fact, try to gather support for such a move, but he was largely ignored. Peary fretted in his cabin and had a compass installed to make sure they were heading in the right direction. When anything interesting happened, Jo would hold her hand mirror up to the transom so that Bert could see a little of the action on deck. Two weeks passed in this misery until finally the *Kite* reached its destination, McCormick Bay.

Jo went over the side of the ship and walked around, getting her land legs and scouting for a place to build their house. She picked a small knoll, drawn to its carpeting of dark green moss strewn with white, pink, and yellow flowers. In the background were red sandstone cliffs about 1,800 feet high, holding back the ice cap.

The house would take some days to build, so a tent was set up on the beach for the Pearys. Everyone else stayed aboard the ship. Bert, strapped to a board, was taken off the ship like cargo—not a great beginning for an explorer. Jo's first night in that tent, lying wide awake beside her sleeping husband, was one of terror. The wind whistled and roared, the flimsy canvas tent creaked and flapped in response, and something out there was bellowing and blowing. Jo didn't have a gun for protection, her husband was helpless and, worse, sleeping peacefully through all this. She wouldn't dream of waking him; she had to prove how brave she could be. It was a long, and long-remembered, night. The next day Jo found out that the noises had come from a school of whales cavorting in the bay and of no possible danger.

Jo was so tired from unpacking and acting as nurse for her husband and as housekeeper and cook for the expedition that she slept through the leave-taking of the *Kite* and its passengers a few days later. She probably wished she had sailed south with them when, that same afternoon, a terrible rainstorm sent a constant stream of water flooding through the tent. She had to sit cross-legged for hours on top of the crates where Bert lay. Jo found out the hard way that rain in the Arctic could be as difficult as snow. Only a few inches below the surface the ground is permanently frozen. Called permafrost, it cannot absorb rain or large amounts of meltwater from ice. The result is a rushing flood stream or, in depressions, a pond like the ones that Bert and Christian Maigaard had encountered on the ice cap.

Despite the fact that it rained every day, the Peary house was finished by the end of the week. They named it Redcliffe—Jo's spelling; Bert spelled it "Red Cliff." Seven feet high, it was constructed of boards covered by tar paper inside and out and lined with heavy cardboard. Red blanketing covered the inner walls and ceilings. A stone wall about four feet from the house was topped by boxes of provisions, which were in turn covered by canvas that was stretched over to the roof of the house and secured. Thus there was a protected area that helped insulate the house and in which they could leave wet clothing, snowshoes, and skis. Snow igloos served as storehouses and would house the Eskimos when they joined the compound.

Redcliffe had two rooms—a bedroom for the Pearys about $7\frac{1}{2}$ feet by 12 feet and furnished by Jo with a double bed and rug she had brought with her, and a living room about twice that size with bunk beds built in against one wall for the men— "the boys," as the Pearys always called expedition members. The stove sat in the wall between the two rooms, heating both: Jo reassured her family that the temperature never fell below 16 degrees— Fahrenheit. She described her usual in-house costume: "a knit kidney protector, a Jaro combination suit, two knit skirts, a flannel wrapper, and a pair of knit stockings, together with a pair of deerskin ones."

The rain did not stop until August 8, Matt Henson's birthday. It was the celebrant's privilege to choose the menu for dinner, and that night Jo prepared Matt's choices: soup, stew of little auk (a local diving bird) with green peas, breaded breast of eider duck (also local), baked beans (Boston), corn, tomatoes, apricot pie, sliced peaches, and coffee. Matt himself made a plum duff, a dessert he learned to make from the cook on board the *Kite*. Peary, who that same day had been released from the box that protected his leg and fitted with splints that allowed him to get around on crutches fashioned by Dr. Cook, served cocktails made from a secret Peary recipe with two kinds of wine. Jo wrote in her diary that night, "A merrier party never sat down to a table anywhere."

On August 11, there was another feast for the Peary's third wedding anniversary. This was not exactly living Eskimo-style, as Bert had theorized. Actually, there were no Eskimos. So the men— except Matt, whom Jo wanted with her for protection—went by boat to nearby Northumberland Island to find some. At the end of a week, they returned with a man named Ikwa and his wife, Mane. (The spellings of these and other Eskimo names are those used most frequently by Peary; there are many variant spellings, no one of which seems to be definitive.) The Eskimos, with their two babies, came out of curiosity and liked what they saw, so they stayed. Other families soon followed, enticed by the oddity of it all and the promise of food and gifts.

Everyone settled into a routine. Peary, still a naval officer, ran the expedition with a touch of the military: watches were kept day and night. They were changed every four hours at first, but when the men complained they could get no rest with such a schedule, the watch was extended to twelve hours. The Eskimos taught the men to hunt, handle dogs, and use skis; they doubled up with laughter at the ineptness of their pupils. When the weather was bad, they all worked in the living room on their sledges and skis, their collections of rocks, or the photographs and data on the physiognomy of the Eskimos.

Jo's day started with coffee in bed for herself and Bert. Then she did the housekeeping and prepared lunch "for my family." In the afternoon she took walks, sometimes did a little shooting, read, and started dinner at four. She did a lot of sewing: "Mr. Peary gives me an idea of what kind of garment he wants, and I [make] experimental outfits out of . . . flannel, which, when satisfactory, will be used as patterns by which the skins will be cut, this avoiding . . . wasting any of the valuable furs."[2]

The furs were prepared and sewn into garments by the Eskimo women. First the skins were scraped with a knife; then they were stretched tight and allowed to dry, after which the women chewed and sucked them to get out the fat. Once again the skins were allowed to dry, and then they were scraped again, this time with a dull blade, to break the fibers down still further and make the skins pliable. A woman could chew two large skins a day, but she had to rest her jaws every other day. When they were ready to sew the skins, the women would take off their kamiks (snow boots that reached high on their thighs) and sit in their fur shorts with their bare legs stretched out in front of them. (If they felt warm, their tops would come off, too.) They would grip one end of the skin between their toes and draw the skin taut. Then, working down toward their toes, they would use an ivory or bone needle holding thread made of sinew to whipstitch a seam.

Jo admired the Eskimo women. Without their sewing skills, survival in the Arctic would not have been possible. She was impressed by their industriousness and considered them her friends, but she preferred to stay at a distance. "I dislike very much to have the Eskimos in my room on account of their dirty condition, and especially as they are alive with parasites of which I am in deadly fear, much to the amusement of our party."[3] Jo was much criticized over the years for her "elitist" attitude toward the Eskimo women. But by parasites, Jo meant lice, and while lice were not uncommon in the nineteenth century, it hardly seems fair that Jo should be faulted because she did not want to be infested with them. The men had to accept them as a way of life, because the lice stayed in their fur clothing and were hard to get out. But Jo did her best to keep them off Bert by rubbing him—and herself—with alcohol every night.

On Christmas that year, Jo prepared a dinner for the Eskimos (whom they called "huskies") of milk punch, venison stew with corn bread, biscuits (cookies), coffee, candy, and raisins. The expedition members ate the same meal, with the addition of salmon "à la can," rabbit pie, plum pudding, and apricot pie. They exchanged small gifts. Jo's gift to Bert was a guidon, a small flag she had made of silk for him to carry on his journeys. Bert gave Jo two hairpins he had carved himself. On New Year's Day, 1892, there was a repeat of the festivities for both the expedition and the Eskimos.

By mid-January Bert was able to take his first outing on snowshoes. But not long afterward, he was a patient again, as "la grippe," which we now call the flu, swept through the expedition members. Fortunately, the Eskimos escaped, or they might have died, having little resistance to foreign diseases. Bert was a peevish and difficult patient and kept Jo busy day and night. She wrote in her diary at the beginning of April, "For the first time since I have known him, he has the blues, and pretty badly at that. He has lost confidence in himself, and is harder to nurse than after his accident aboard the *Kite*. . . . I saw that he was very much exhausted, and I gave him his salt-water sponge-bath under the blankets, after which he slept very well, something he had not done of late."[4] That sponge bath must have been just what the doctor ordered, for just two days later Peary, Astrup, and the Eskimo Annowkah sledged across the bay to Herbert Island to get blubber they had stored there during the summer. Sledging actually meant a twenty-five-mile jog, since only supplies or the sick or injured rode.

By the end of April the party had traded for twenty-two good dogs and were ready to start the ice cap expedition. Henson, Cook, Gibson, and Astrup started ahead, to be followed later by Peary. Henson soon came back for additional equipment and went out again with Peary, only to return for good a few days later with a frozen heel. Then Gibson returned, followed by Cook. Only Peary and Astrup remained. They moved mostly northeast until, fifty-seven days into the journey, they stepped off the ice cap and onto rocky red-brown land dotted with snowdrifts. They had crossed the Greenland ice cap. The men left the sleds and dogs and backpacked to the north, where they became the first individuals to look upon a great bay beside a towering cliff. Peary's dream. It was July 4, and Peary named the cliff Navy Cliff, and the bay Independence Bay. He marked them with a piece of Jo's guidon. There were yellow poppies and dandelions in bloom, and bees were buzzing about in this ice-free far northern part of Greenland, which would bear the name Peary Land.

Peary saw a cleft in a distant range of mountains to the west and thought that Independence Bay extended through it to the Arctic Sea. Actually, the bay did not empty into the cleft; it turned eastward and emptied into the Greenland Sea. This mistake was easy to make from where Peary stood, as explorers following him discovered. The first of these, the Danish explorer Ludvig Mylius-Erichsen and two other men, went to the area in May 1907, found the error, and drew corrected maps. What happened then is something of a mystery. The party could not traverse the sea ice because it was too soft, and so they went onto the inland ice. They died there of starvation and frostbite in the twenty-four-hour night of November. What had they been doing all that time? If the sea ice was too soft, their move onto the ice cap must have been in August or early September at the latest; the ice would have frozen after that. They knew where they were and where they were going—their corrected maps were found with the body of the last man to die. Yet Peary's error in geography has been blamed for these deaths.

Astrup and Peary turned back for Redcliffe. They had just enough food for the crossing, and with only three position reckonings, they came within five miles north of where they wanted to be. They corrected course, and in the distance they saw figures moving toward them. Jo, Henson, and Dr. Cook had come out to meet up with them, and there was vast jubilation. Back at Redcliffe, it took a while for the Eskimos to accept the fact that the men and dogs had not been turned into spirits—they believed only spirits could live on the inland ice.

The Eskimos were soon reassured, although their misgivings added some tension to an event that had happened earlier at Redcliffe. While the rest of the expedition was gone, Henson and Gibson thought they overheard the Eskimos plotting to kill them. Jo didn't believe that was possible and felt the men had misunderstood, that they didn't know the

49

Eskimo language well enough. All the same, the men armed themselves. This frightened the Eskimos into believing *they* would be killed, which in turn led back to the possibility of their doing the killing first. Fortunately, nothing came of the incident, but "I am sorry for this episode," Jo was to write. "[It] has brought about an unpleasantness with the Eskimos." Whatever the reality behind the incident, this fear of the Eskimos has been reported on and built up over the decades and is used against Peary to this day, although he was not even there when it occurred. If at any time the Eskimos had been deeply frightened, they would have killed one or more of the party. At the very least, their best men would not have worked for Peary as they did. The Eskimos gave their help freely and generously, but only to those whom they respected.

The Eskimos did hate Verhoeff, who was arrogant to them—and to everyone else. Perhaps he was simply unable to adapt to the close quarters and the isolation of life in the Far North. He was sure they would run out of coal and freeze to death, and when he was on watch, he used so little of it to keep the fire burning that Jo was miserable. In his diary he referred to Henson as a "nigger," and he resented the man's equal status on the expedition team. Verhoeff also hated taking orders. Warned repeatedly not to go more than 500 yards from the house by himself, he repeatedly ignored the warning. One day, shortly before the expedition was due to leave for home, Verhoeff did not return. No one knows whether he fell into a crevasse or the Eskimos killed him, for his body was never found. Search parties spent days scouring the area for dozens of miles around, but they found only a few rock specimens piled beside a glacier. This suggested that Verhoeff might have been there and fallen into one of the many crevasses nearby. Despite their conviction that he was dead, Peary left a year's supply of food at Cairn Point, where supplies were cached for emergencies. If Verhoeff had somehow wandered out of any search party's range and actually survived, he would know to look there for food.

The time had come for the North Greenland Expedition to return to the United States. The entire expedition helped the Eskimos hunt walrus, musk oxen, and other game so that they would have enough supplies for the winter. This was a custom Peary would always follow at the beginning and end of an expedition to ensure that the Eskimos would not suffer any deprivation for having joined him. Then the Pearys handed out pots, kettles, thimbles, knives, needles, and all kinds of hardware and lumber to the Eskimos. Jo worried about them anyway: "Have these poor ignorant people, who are absolutely isolated from the rest of humanity, really benefited from their intercourse with us or have we only opened their eyes to their desolate condition? I hope the latter is not the case, for a happier, merrier set of people I have never seen."[5]

Jo worried about giving the Eskimos too much, but future critics would fault the expedition for giving too little and for not offering money or some sort of ongoing support. The critics were and are apparently unaware that the Greenland Eskimos at that time had no form of money, and did not use money, and that the prevailing philosophy was not to interfere with the natural development of life among these people. Those items that seem so small to Peary's detractors were of tremendous value to the Eskimos. They had plenty of furs and could always get more. But lumber? Saws? Nails? Mirrors? These were far more valuable to them than thousands of gold pieces.

As their reward, the members of the expedition received some furs and ivories, but their greatest rewards were to be found within themselves, in their pride in the adventure, in their knowledge of a job well done, and in the thrill of having seen places that had never before been seen. For Peary, the reward was considerable, a dream come true: "Neither gold nor fame, nor aught can purchase from me the supreme memory of the moment, when on the ice cap, far above the earth, with the rustling of the Stars and Stripes in my ears, I laughed with the laughing waves of the great white sea in greeting to the returning sun."[6]

IV

THE
SNOW BABY

On August 3, 1893, Bert and Jo, who was pregnant, returned to Greenland. They were famous now, but getting back to Greenland had not been easy. Peary could not get government funding, and he had a hard time getting leave. But he had learned how to play the game better. He had turned to friends in high places: the head of the Philadelphia Academy of Sciences, who had petitioned the Secretary of the Navy on Bert's behalf and had won him three years' leave. To earn funds for the trip, Jo had written a book about her year in Greenland, and Bert had returned to the lecture circuit.

Peary had secured the services of an agent to get him bookings. He and Matt Henson had traveled around the country, bringing with them the props necessary for a good show—a sledge, snowshoes, harpoons. Henson would demonstrate, perspiring madly in his fur clothes, as Peary lectured. They gave 165 shows in 103 days and earned $20,000. After deducting expenses, including salary for Henson and two secretaries, Peary had $13,000 left for the expedition. That wasn't enough, so he had made an attraction of the ship that was going to take them to the Arctic. At a quarter a head, in ports from Philadelphia to Portland, he collected the money he needed. If he felt bitter about having to make a showman of himself, he didn't dwell on it. But he did become a lot shrewder about money—another point that his detractors have held against him.

Bert devoted much time to choosing the people to accompany him in this assault on the Greenland ice cap. The close quarters and enforced togetherness of an expedition required a compatible crew to be completely successful. He chose Henson, of course, and Astrup and Dr. Cook from the previous trip. Cook later decided not to go, however, and was replaced as surgeon by Dr. Edwin E. Vincent. Samuel J. Entrikin became Peary's first assistant, and Evelyn Briggs Baldwin was named meteorologist. The others were Hugh J. Lee, George F. Clark, George H. Carr, James Davidson, and Wallace F. Swain, all of whom received the title of assistant. Frederick Stokes, an artist, paid for his passage. Stokes would set up his own cabin close to the group quarters but he did not contribute money to the expedition, as Verhoeff had. Peary did not want any more problems with someone who might refuse to obey orders because he had helped underwrite the cost of the expedition. A nurse, Susan J. Cross, was also hired to accompany the party for Jo's sake.

Except for Henson, each expedition member had to sign a contract acknowledging Peary as leader and agreeing to follow his directions. The contract also stipulated that they turn over their diaries and notes at the end of the expedition and that they would not lecture or publish books about the trip. Peary wanted no competition for the book and articles he planned to write and the lecture tours he would undertake for future financing. After all, that was the only way an explorer mounting an expensive expedition was remunerated. Peary agreed to provide transportation, equipment, a rifle and ammunition, a knife, and a small salary for each of the men.

Peary's first efforts on landing in Greenland were directed toward anxious questioning of the Eskimos for news of Verhoeff. The Eskimos were silent—it was their custom not to speak of the dead. That upset the members of the expedition, which from the first did not go well. Astrup came down with a severe stomach ailment, and George Carr slipped on ice and hurt his back. The homing pigeons they had hoped to use for sending messages from the ice cap were eaten almost immediately by the Eskimo dogs, which were notorious for eating everything in sight. Most of the homing pigeons that did get aloft were eaten in flight by ravens. Only one succeeded in bringing a message back. This was of little value, however, since the bird had been sent out at the very start of the trek across the ice cap. Peary had brought some burros along to see how they would fare in carrying supplies, but they didn't get past the voracious dogs, either. When Astrup and some others took supplies to the ice cap to cache them for the following spring's journey, they could not do the job as well as they had hoped. And a huge iceberg calved (broke away) from neighboring Bowdoin Glacier and caused a tidal wave that swamped or smashed three boats on the beach and carried away all of their barrels of oil. Peary had hoped to use the oil to generate electricity for light and heat for their new base, called Anniversary

Lodge in honor of the Pearys' fifth wedding anniversary, which was celebrated a few days after they arrived. A full day of trying to retrieve the bobbing barrels from the sea exhausted the men, and still much of the oil was lost. It was an annoyance more than anything else, however—just another trapping of civilization they would have to do without.

One of the few bright spots during the expedition was the birth of Marie Ahnighito Peary on September 12, 1893. The name Marie was for an aunt, and Ahnighito, a name the Pearys liked, was that of an Eskimo woman. The Eskimos were enchanted by this first white baby they had seen. Jo wrote, "She was the source of the liveliest interest to the Eskimos. Entire families journeyed from far away to satisfy themselves by actual touch that she was really a creature of warm flesh and blood, and not of snow, as they at first believed."[1] To the world, little Marie Ahnighito became the Snow Baby. (Ninety-five years later, a famous New York City department store would offer Snow Baby dolls modeled after little Marie.) Peary, however, was terrified of the little baby and refused to hold her until she was three weeks old. Jo was distraught over this. "Bert don't like my baby," she told one of the members of the party, probably Mrs. Cross. Jo was far from home, without the reassurance of family and friends, and she feared that if she died the baby would be left to starve. Surreptitiously, she got the baby accustomed to drinking from a bottle so that she would not need to be breast-fed. As it turned out, however, little Ahnighito was a healthy, happy baby who thrived, and so did Jo.

The men kept on with their preparations for crossing the ice cap in the spring, preparations that were much like those of the previous expedition. Peary planned to go to Independence Bay with a party of eight men. Three men would then turn northward across the bay to search for the top of Greenland, which, for all he knew, might turn out to be the top of the world, the North Pole. Another three-man party would go south from Independence Bay to map the east coast of Greenland. The remaining two men would hunt the musk oxen seen on the previous trip, so that when all the parties rejoined one another, there would be fresh meat for the return journey. The plan was a good one, but in the execution, it turned into a shambles.

At the very outset, Astrup's stomach acted up again, and Hugh Lee's toes were frozen. Peary and George Clark had to accompany the two men back to Anniversary Lodge, then hustle to catch up with the expedition. Soon after, a terrible windstorm, common on the ice cap, with temperatures of −40°F, brought the dogs to a halt. The men put up two tents, but Peary wrote in his diary that the drift "was almost indescribable" and forced the men out of one of the tents lest they be suffocated by the snow. They moved into the other tent, but drift soon narrowed this space, too. The men had to lie down and curl up, and one man at a time would take his turn standing, hanging on to the tent pole.

The next morning the wind subsided and Peary looked "upon a scene that made me sick at heart. Half my dogs were frozen fast in the snow, some by the legs, and all were in a most pitiable condition, their fur a mass of ice and snow driven into it by the pitiless wind."[2] Baldwin, the meteorologist, checked his instruments, which showed that over a thirty-four-hour period, the wind had averaged over 48 miles an hour and the temperature had dipped to a low of −60°F. Peary believed that the storm held the record as "the most severe ever experienced by an Arctic party."

Davidson had suffered frostbite on his heel and was sent back to Anniversary Lodge along with the surgeon; Peary felt that by this time there was more need for a doctor at the lodge than on the ice cap. Clark, with three fingers and a toe frostbitten, chose to go on with Peary, Henson, Entrikin, and Baldwin. Traveling was extremely difficult as sledges slid and crashed on *sastrugi,* ridges of packed snow with the consistency of slick marble, frozen swells in a sea of ice. The weakest dogs were put out of their misery and used as food to strengthen the other dogs. Then one of the dogs started biting the rest. It had gone *piblockto,* suffered a kind of madness, and although this was not an infectious or contagious disease like rabies or distemper, the dog had to be shot to protect the other dogs. *Piblockto* took many forms and afflicted not only the dogs but also the Eskimos, particularly the women, who recovered spontaneously as long as they were protected against harming themselves.

Entrikin froze the soles of his feet and hurt his back, Clark froze his nose, and then came another two-day storm. More dead dogs, more *piblockto.* Peary finally ordered a return to Anniversary Lodge. The party had traveled only 128 miles in three weeks. In contrast, the return trip took only ten days, even though they were delayed by Peary's and Clark's snow blindness and Clark's frostbitten feet. To make them even more miserable, they were covered with lice, which thrived in the fur clothing they had not been able to take off for over a month.

It took weeks for the men to recover. Jo did not make her feelings known publicly, but she must have been dismayed, as Bert's mother had been, at the forces that drove this man to endure such hardships.

While Bert was recuperating, Jo and he took off

on a sledging trip to map a nearby bay some fifty miles long. This was Jo's first sledge trip, and apparently it was the only time she and Bert had alone together. Little Ahnighito was in good hands with Mrs. Cross and Miss Bill, a twelve-year-old Eskimo girl who served as baby-sitter.

By mid-May, Bert was off again, this time in search of an "iron mountain." In the early 1800s Sir John Ross, one of the great Arctic explorers looking for the Northwest Passage (and discoverer of the Polar Eskimos with whom Peary worked, a group so isolated that they thought they were the only people in the world), brought back with him some metal knives said to have come from a mountain. Tests showed that the metal had to be from a meteorite, but only the Eskimos knew where it was, and they weren't about to tell. They didn't want to lose this magical source that provided them with metal for knives and harpoon blades.

By Peary's time, though, the Eskimos no longer needed the meteorite iron, since they traded for or were given knives by the long line of explorers and whalers who were constantly coming into their lands. One of the Eskimos was willing to take Peary and Hugh Lee to the site, and they made their way south along the sea ice. Their guide soon deserted them, but Peary and Lee found another, Tallakoteah, at a small village. Tallakoteah told them of three "great irons," or *saviksue.* The Eskimos believed that these "irons" used to be a woman and her dog who lived in a tent in the sky but who were thrown to the ground by an evil spirit, which turned them into iron. Peary interpreted this to mean that ancient Eskimos had seen the meteorites fall, but scientists who analyzed the meteorites later refuted this. All three pieces were found to be from one meteorite that broke apart in the upper atmosphere (more pieces have since been found) and fell to earth long before the Eskimos reached the area.

The three men continued south in what Peary said was one of the most difficult trips he had ever made. He had never traveled over sea ice before, but in Greenland, where mountains reach into the sea, it was the only way north or south. It was late spring, and the sea ice was particularly difficult, obstructed by giant slabs that had piled up on one another as tides slammed them against the shore. Farther out the ice was broken, slushy, and covered with deep snow. When the sea ice became impassable, the party retreated to the mountainous shore and climbed up and over and down, carrying or dragging sledges, supplies, and pulling dogs. But Tallakoteah finally led them to the great irons. Under the snow, he located first the pile of stones the Eskimos had used to flake off and shape pieces of the meteorites. Then, using a snow knife—a slightly curved, blunt ivory implement about two inches wide and a foot long—he dug down and uncovered "the Woman." "The Tent" and "the Dog" were nearby.

Peary claimed the meteorites by right of discovery and left a message to that effect in a cairn built of rocks, the usual message or signal center in the Arctic. He would later return with the ship and the equipment to move the tremendously heavy meteorites, whose density made them far heavier than boulders of the same size. The ethics of the day did not militate against removing archaeological, ethnological, and artistic items from their country of origin. Peary felt the meteorites warranted study by scientists. The Danes had laid no claim to them; the Eskimos no longer needed them, nor did they revere the stones, as some people have said. They did hold the stones in awe, but Peary saw that as nothing more than superstition. He saw no difference between those objects and the small rocks and botanical specimens the various museums had wanted him to bring back as scientific curiosities. He might have offered payment for them, but to whom? And what kind of payment? He also recognized, of course, their value to him as products to be sold to the highest museum bidder.

The return to Anniversary Lodge was a nightmare. The ice kept breaking up, forcing the men to travel on land time and again. The most horrendous part of the trip was a sixty-mile-an-hour sledge ride down a glacier, with the men using their bodies as rudders and brakes. Lee was unable to open his eyes to steer for more than a second at a time because of snow blindness, and Peary, who was suffering the aftereffects of rotten walrus meat he had eaten in desperation when they ran out of other food, was barely conscious.

But somehow, once again, they survived, and they made it home.

In late July 1894 the Eskimos brought word that the expedition's ship, the *Falcon*, was icebound to the south. Entrikin struck out for the ship and brought back with him Emil Diebitsch, Jo's brother, with a family message that Jo and little Marie were to come home! It was late August before the *Falcon* finally broke through the ice and reached Anniversary Lodge, where it picked up its return passengers, including Jo, the baby, and Miss Bill—who wanted to see the world.

Peary, Henson, and Hugh Lee were staying in Greenland. They wanted another try at crossing the inland ice. Bert went down the coast with Jo on the *Falcon*, but left to take a whaleboat back north that allowed him to make a careful map of the coastline. It would be Jo and Bert's first long separation. Jo could hardly handle the short ones; how would she manage for a year? She was to find that staying safe at home had little to commend it. "I have come to the conclusion," she would one day say, "that it is easier to go to the Arctic and do the things you are interested in and content to do than it is to stay at home, bring up the children, fight your husband's battles, and look out for the bread and butter for the family. I think hereafter I will do the exploring and let Mr. Peary take care of home life."[3] Alas, that was not to be, and Jo would for many years have to "look out for the bread and butter."

After the departure of the ship, Hugh Lee suffered a bad case of homesickness. To get his mind off home, Peary sent him out hunting with Matt Henson. The two men then went to the ice cap to check on the giant cache of food and supplies that had been left there the year before. They brought back bad news. They had gone as far as the first cache and found it buried so deep in snow that they couldn't reach it. The pemmican, biscuits, milk, pea soup, cranberry jam, and fuel alcohol were lost. They had left the supplies they had on them, but that would hardly be sufficient for the spring expedition. In addition to this blow, Peary had trouble getting dogs from the Eskimos. He learned that Astrup had told the Eskimos to hold the dogs for his return to Greenland on his own expedition in a year or two, when he would pay one rifle for every two dogs. Peary was furious. He could not match this offer, and he bitterly resented the competition from one of his "boys." Eventually, however, he was able to buy thirty-five dogs and rent thirty more.

Peary was dejected. On the eve of their departure for the inland ice at the end of March 1895, he wrote to Jo, knowing she would not receive the letter for many months. He told her about Astrup and his plans for the expedition, and made a settlement of his affairs.

I owe each [of two Eskimos] a gun. The others I have settled with. I have a sledge contracted for with Poodloanah for Chopsie [Marie Ahnighito] and I have a standing offer of a flask of powder for a young bearskin for her. Of the three narwhal heads and tusks [ivory] on the roof, one for Emil, whose kindness I shall always remember, one for Bridgman [a Brooklyn newspaper editor], who is more than thoughtful, and . . . the other for you. . . . Papers and records . . . in the steamer trunk and the two lock . . . boxes. These, with the ammunition, are under the floor of our room. . . .Two of the guns are also under the floor, three behind the books and your shotgun in one of the closets. One shotgun and one carbine I have loaned to Nuktah. . . . I have promised him Stokes' house. The other three men . . . I have promised . . . [a] portion of the house [Anniversary Lodge]. . . . The rest of the house . . . put on exhibition, it will make you independent. . . . All the keys I have put back of the books on the very top shelf. Good-by my darling.[4]

The three men had cut their hair very short and aired their fur clothes to minimize the plague of lice. They bathed and shaved, and on the morning of April 1, a Monday, they climbed up to the ice cap. Despite their fear of demons, four Eskimos went with them to help bring up supplies. When another exhaustive search failed to turn up the previous year's cache, Peary asked for a vote about continuing the expedition. He explained that they would have supplies only for the journey out. Before heading back, they would have to find game in the Independence Bay region, as he and Henson had done before. But there were no guarantees that the musk oxen would still be there. Once having had the experience of being shot at, they might have moved on. Still, Lee and Henson voted to go on.

Before the men traveled too far in, Peary sent the Eskimos back. He worried deeply about them, knowing they would have to find their way back under the additional burden of their terrible fear of the ice cap. Soon, though, there were other things for him to worry about. Hugh Lee, who was to care for the dogs, took sick, and the dogs attacked the evening's ration of walrus meat and Peary and Henson as well. Then a blizzard kept the party holed up for two days. Lee's sledge was demolished on rough ice, and a frozen toe caused him great pain. By the first week in May the party had only eleven dogs left, Lee was in bad shape, and they all faced starvation. But in the distance they saw land. And land meant game. Peary made Lee as comfortable as possible and left the dogs with him. Then he and Henson headed for and soon reached the land, but they found no game. They went back to Lee, put him in a more secure spot, took the dogs, and tried again. Nothing. Then suddenly they spotted a snow hare! They shot it, cooked it, devoured it—and were hungrier than before. The next morning they finally found the herd of musk oxen, and their lives were saved.

Henson went back with meat for Hugh Lee while Peary stayed and took observations of the area, correcting his first map. In the distance, he saw a distinctive mountain, which he named Mount Wistar. This and other landmarks seen from a variety of places at future times were to establish Greenland as an island, with ocean between it and the top of the world. Peary also made the first observations of the peculiarities of wind direction on the ice cap, which eventually led to the realization that Green-

The young Robert Peary

Matthew Henson on his first journey north

Redcliffe house and the Pearys' tent

Josephine Peary—and the trappings of civilization—with Ikwa,
Mane, and children. Note the baby in Mane's hood.

Anniversary Lodge

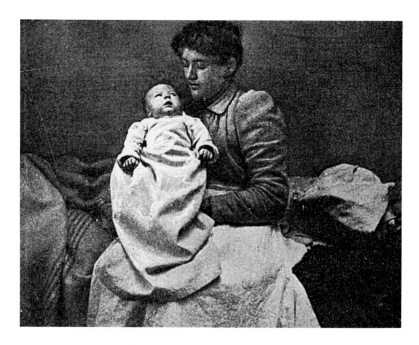

Josephine Peary and
the Snow Baby

Coaxing at one end and pushing at the other
to get sledges over hummocks

A sledge on dry land is like a boat out of water.

Man joins dogs in the traces to exert all their might to move this load.

After the storm

Note the dog buried in snow.

The largest meteorite ever found being loaded
via a special bridge which was designed and built by Peary

Musk oxen herd east of an ice cap. These animals graze
in the same place year after year, as is proved by
the skeletal remains of previous grazers in the foreground.

Marie Ahnighito and friend

The Peary expedition hut at Cape Sabine

The dogs have been released from this sledge
for fear of their being harmed if the sledge overran
them on the perilous way down.

land was the weather factory for northern Europe. (Later, during World War II, the Germans and then the Americans used Greenland's ice cap to monitor wind and weather for military purposes in Europe.)

The men did little further exploration. They had to get back across the ice cap with only nine dogs left to pull sledges. They fed the musk oxen meat to the dogs to give them strength, and the men ate biscuits. Eight days into the return trip, Hugh Lee dropped to the ice, too weak to continue. Peary and Henson turned back to help, and Lee told them to leave him and save themselves. "We will all get home or none of us will," Peary replied. They made camp and nursed Lee with warm milk laced with beef extract and brandy until he felt better. They started up again the next day in a battle against time. Some dogs died, and other dogs were shot for food for the remaining dogs and for the men. They were down to one dog when the coastline came into view. A short while later, they were in Anniversary Lodge. The dog was too exhausted to make it all the way, but the men did, knowing the dog would follow when it could.

And when it did, Peary fed the dog by hand, limiting its rations. But the men couldn't handle even the smallest amounts of food. Violent stomach cramps and diarrhea debilitated them even further. Virtually unconscious, Peary thought he heard Henson and Lee talking about poison, and the word haunted him. Later he tasted a cake Henson had made and thought it bitter; he would not eat it. This was the kind of craziness brought on by extreme weakness, Peary reasoned. Then again, he thought, seven leaders of Arctic expeditions were known to have been killed by mutineers, and he had not been able to inspire the love and loyalty of his men—his "boys"—as he had hoped. The tinge of suspicion seems to have stayed with him for a long while, affecting his easy relationship with Matt Henson.

Then the *Kite* arrived, with Emil Diebitsch aboard. Jo had raised the money to send the ship on a "Peary Relief Expedition" with supplies for the three men. She had done things she hated to get the money: she pleaded with the directors of science associations and of museums, she lectured, and she used family money. Peary hadn't even bothered to arrange for a ship to bring supplies—he had no doubt that a ship would reach him, and with good reason—Jo.

One of the contributors to the Peary Relief Expedition was the American Museum of Natural History in New York City, which offered to assist with the meteorites, too. The *Kite* headed south to pick them up. The Dog and the Woman were hoisted aboard, but it was impossible to move the Tent. Special equipment and all of Peary's engineering skills were needed to get it aboard a ship on another expedition in 1897. (The Tent, christened Ahnighito by little Marie Ahnighito Peary, was so heavy that twenty-four horses strained to pull the specially built wagon carrying it to the museum, and the wheels of the wagon carved ruts in the roadway. But that was years later, after the meteorite had sat in storage at the Brooklyn Navy Yard for some years. And it was Jo who negotiated the price— $40,000, a very good sum for the time, especially since the museum already had the meteorites on display. They are still there, and Ahnighito is still the largest meteorite ever found.)

Along with the meteorite, Peary brought back six Eskimos who wanted to see the world. (Or perhaps Peary wanted the world to see them, a deplorable custom explorers had picked up from the days when they brought home natives to prove they had gotten where they said they had.) Unfortunately, four of the Eskimo men died of tuberculosis, which was pandemic in those days. The fifth, the young son of one of the dead men, was adopted by a Museum of Natural History staff member and did not return to Greenland until many years later. He worked with the explorer Donald MacMillan for a number of years and returned to the United States in 1916, only to die two years later in the great influenza epidemic. The Eskimo who survived, Uisakavsak, returned to his village, where he told of igloos as high as icebergs and giant dogs (horses), and puffing iron sledges that moved without dogs pulling them and carried as many people as lived in this village. When he told of talking to Peary in the next village through a box, his people had heard enough. "Go tell your lies to the women," they said, and renamed him the Big Liar. So Uisakavsak left the village, and because he was a very good hunter, he became very rich.

But that was later. Now the ship was bringing home a dejected and unnerved Peary who thought of himself as a failure. The world thought differently and hailed him as a hero; the American Geographical Society and the Royal Geographic Society of London awarded Peary gold medals. His self-esteem and natural sense of optimism soon revived, and once again he was ready to do battle. This time Robert Edwin Peary would reach for one of the greatest prizes of all—the North Pole.

MATTERS
OF LIVING
AND
DYING

Starvation, frostbite, snow blindness, exhaustion—
how could a man expose himself to all this? For
Robert Peary the choice was simple: he could do
nothing else. His drive was as strong as the lem-
mings' drive to reach the sea and drown in it.

Peary's plan for reaching the Pole was much as
he had outlined it years before in Philadelphia when
he had haunted the bookstores in search of material
on the Arctic. He called it the "Peary route": he
would take a ship through the Davis Strait and into
Smith Sound, sailing as far north as the ice permitted; then he would get out and walk. And what a
walk that would be!

How would he know when he got there? The Pole
is at latitude 90° north, so he would take latitude
readings until he reached 90° north, or as close to
that as possible. No one knew what was at the Pole
or what it would be like. Some people thought it

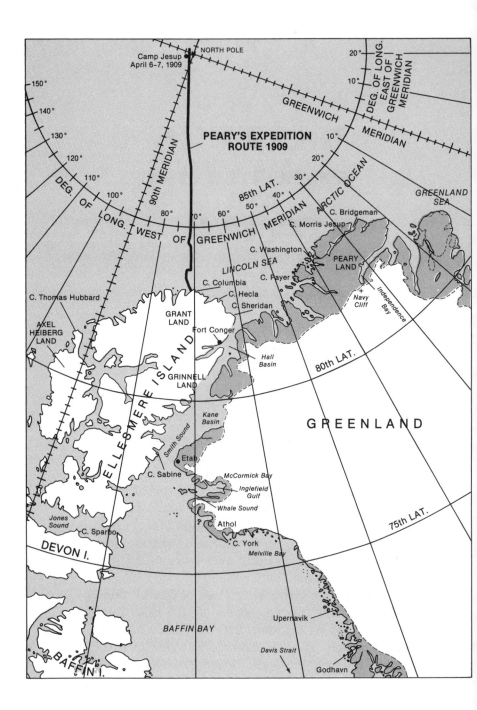

would be a great hole or an island or an Atlantis—something tangible. But Peary understood that the Pole is nothing but a mathematical point, one end of the imaginary line that is the axis about which the earth revolves. It is a point that moves about slightly in response to forces within the earth. (It can be computed with a high degree of accuracy only from a satellite, and that kind of accuracy belonged to a later time than Peary's.) There were other instruments of measurement even in his time, but they could not be used in the primitive conditions and low temperatures that he faced. Peary would not even bother to take longitude readings since the equipment was cumbersome and the process long. All lines of longitude converge at the Poles, and it mattered little which one he was on as long as he was on or close to 90° north latitude.

He needed a ship, he needed money, and he needed more leave from the Navy. The last proved the hardest. The Navy wanted Peary to behave like a proper naval lieutenant; so far, he had spent most of his time on leave. He tried making explanations and using influence, but nothing worked. The Navy was preparing for possible war with Spain, and Lieutenant Peary was ordered to duty at Mare Island on the west coast, and that was that. Or so thought the Navy. When the Spanish-American War finally broke out in 1898, Lieutenant Peary was in the Arctic. He had reached there through the good services of a man named Charles A. Moore. Moore was a strong supporter of Peary and also of the new president of the United States, William McKinley. A friendly visit to the president by Moore had resulted in the cancellation of Peary's orders and the granting of a five-year leave from the Navy.

New sources also helped fund this expedition. Morris K. Jesup, railroad magnate, banker, and president of both the American Geographical Society and the American Museum of Natural History, had become interested in Arctic exploration when Jo approached him for funds for the Peary Relief Expedition. Jesup wanted Eskimo artifacts for the museum, but he also liked Peary and knew what it meant to want desperately to do something but not have the money for it. Jesup had only a sixth-grade education and had worked his way up from destitution to great wealth and power. He called a few of his friends together—later they were to call themselves the Peary Arctic Club—and asked them for pledges of $4,000 each to finance half of an expedition, with Peary raising the rest of the money. An English newspaper publisher, Lord Northcliffe, donated a steam yacht, the *Windward*, whose engines would be beefed up for icebreaking.

Everything looked good until a machinists' strike delayed the engine overhaul and the outbreak of the Spanish American War threatened the financing. Peary became increasingly anxious. The Norwegian explorer Otto Sverdrup was rumored (untruthfully) to be planning the same approach to the Pole, despite Peary's publication of his plans and contrary to the unwritten code of the explorer. And the clock was ticking away Peary's leave. He decided he had enough financing to allow him to charter a ship, the *Hope*, and not wait for the *Windward*.

We can only guess that Jo was less than happy with this turn of events, which meant more years of separation from her husband; nothing was really said about it. On the surface, she wanted what Bert wanted, and she also knew that somehow he would always get what he wanted, whatever her wishes. Peary's ability to get what he wanted was more than luck, although that, too, played a part. It was a result of determination, drive, an informed intelligence, and an inner fire. He might never get the brass ring, but he would keep jumping on the merry-go-round for another try at it. Why Matt Henson kept jumping on with him is anybody's guess; it was a death-defying ride, and Henson couldn't even grab for the brass ring. But the Arctic often captures the heart and the imagination, and perhaps for Matt Henson the ride was everything.

Peary took only two men with him on this expedition: Henson and a surgeon, T. S. Dedrick, Jr., intending to use the highly regarded skills of the Polar Eskimos on the trek to the Pole. On July 3, 1898, as Jo and Bert's mother waved good-bye, the *Hope* sailed for the far north. This time the expedition headed for Etah, high on Greenland's coast, where they would pick up the Polar Eskimo men and their dogs. The *Windward* caught up with them shortly after they arrived at Etah, so Bert sent the *Hope* home and used the *Windward* as his base.

In the fall, Peary sledged westward to Ellesmere Island to map the region. Somehow he happened upon the camp set up by Otto Sverdrup, whom he regarded as a poacher on the Peary Route to the Pole. Sverdrup assured him that he was not going to attempt to reach the Pole, but Peary was not to be placated and refused the invitation to stay for coffee. This was an insult that Sverdrup never forgave, and his enmity in the days ahead would go far toward harming Peary's reputation.

A few weeks after this ominous meeting, Peary, Henson, Dedrick, and the Eskimos left the *Windward* to set up a base at Fort Conger, Adolphus Greely's old base, about 250 miles north. Fort Conger would be their jumping-off place for the spring assault on the Pole. It was now the dead of winter, with a twenty-four-hour night, but a full moon shone for two weeks of every month at those high latitudes. Amplified by the reflection off the mirror-like ice, the moon would give enough light during those weeks for the party to travel by. The trek was horrendous, the winds strong and always blowing against them, and Peary's right arm had mysteriously turned numb. It was so cold that sleep was impossible, and they rested only long enough to make hot tea. But time ran out. They found themselves in total darkness with miles still to go. What if they couldn't find Fort Conger in the dark? It would be two weeks before the moon returned, and meanwhile they could get lost forever in this unexplored land. But Peary's extraordinary skill in translating details from a map into actuality even in the blackness of the Arctic night brought them safely to Fort Conger.

Inside the stone house, in the eerie flickering glow of their small lamps, they saw the room just as the men of the ill-fated Greely expedition had left it fifteen or sixteen years before. It seemed as though those dead men might walk through the doors at any minute and sit down at the table still set with dishes. The room was in chaos, with tins of food, tea, coffee, and biscuits strewn around as if someone had yelled "Fire" or "Abandon ship." The biscuits were still edible—by Arctic explorer standards—and by doubling up the ratio of very stale coffee to a cup of water, they found they could get a creditable brew. They were elated by these extra rations and at having found shelter, even such a ghostly shelter. Peary wrote, "It is doubtful if a more desolate and unsheltered location for a camp could be found anywhere in the Arctic regions, fully exposed to the biting winds from the north, cut off by the rocks back of it from the rays of the southern sun, and besieged by the ice pack surging down from Hall Basin in the north."[1] The site certainly had not been well chosen and had undoubtedly helped lead to the Greely party's demoralization.

For the Peary expedition, there would be trouble of a different kind at Fort Conger. Peary's leg had "a suspicious wooden feeling," and when he removed his kamiks, they saw that all his toes were badly frostbitten. Dr. Dedrick bathed them in ice, as was customary in treating frostbite. But the next day the toes were worse—gangrene had set in and would spread and kill unless at least the worst parts of seven of Bert's toes were amputated immediately. The pain of such an operation in that dark and haunted room can only be imagined. Coupled with the pain, perhaps outstripping it, was the knowledge that Peary might never walk again. Later he was to say, "I never lost faith, in spite of the 'encouraging' statements of my physician that a man who had lost even a big toe could never again walk effectively. I *knew* that I should yet do the work which I had set before myself."[2] Actually, the faith was not to come for some time. The fear was with him from the beginning.

Physical fitness was extremely important to Peary, and not only because he wanted to go exploring. Built into his very being was a need to be manly, pleasing in appearance, strong. Jo said he always walked faster and longer than anyone else, and even at the end of weeks of twenty-mile marches (as days or nights were calculated by Arctic explorers), Bert would be at the head of his men. Now his body was mutilated, his strength depleted. He was crippled.

When winter night ended and the months of mostly twilight set in, Peary was strapped to a sledge and the men set off for Etah. It had taken them several weeks to reach Fort Conger, but they returned to Etah in only eleven days, despite temperatures of −60°F. and the problems of hauling Peary over hummocks (rough hills) of ice. Ahngoodloo, the Eskimo handling his sledge, did a remarkable job, losing control of it only once.

Two weeks after reaching the *Windward*, Bert underwent another operation. Dedrick finished the primitive job he had begun at Fort Conger and removed an eighth toe, leaving Peary with only the little toes on each foot. After a month of recuperating and swinging around on crutches, Peary forced himself to try to walk. Flat-footed, he moved with a gliding motion, but walk he did. He walked farther every day until he was going such distances that he took a sledge to ride on when the pain in his tender stumps made him too sick to his stomach to walk. Finally he was well enough to go with the others to Fort Conger to retrieve Greely's records and then on to map the western shores of Hall Basin.

The summer breakup of the ice brought a relief ship sent by Morris Jesup and the Peary Arctic Club. The secretary of the club, Peary's old friend Herbert L. Bridgman, headed the expedition. He brought a letter from Jo announcing the birth of another daughter, Francine, the previous January. Bert could not know that the child had died five days before the letter reached him.

Peary had another child born about this time, a boy, whose mother was the young, attractive, Allakasingwah. In keeping with his stated theory that women were essential to a healthy expedition, Peary had an ongoing relationship with Allakasingwah. He never acknowledged the relationship; to do so would have been unthinkable in his nineteenth-century world with its Victorian principles of morality. On the other hand, the Eskimos—including Allakasingwah's husband—saw it as entirely natural and acceptable and were proud of the children such unions produced. Matt Henson also had at least one child by an Eskimo woman, and probably most of the other expedition members had, if not children, at least sexual relationships with the women who accompanied them. In a far more sophisticated way, this was Jo's role, too, but Jo's society would not allow its women the freedom the Eskimos gave their women. While Jo would occasionally protest that "life [was] slipping away" without her husband beside her, there was nothing she could or would do about it. Bert lived his dreams, and Jo would wait for hers.

Despite all, and most of all, Bert loved his Arctic world. He sent a letter back with Bridgman for Jo, in which he wrote, "More than once I have taken myself to task for my folly in leaving such a wife and baby (babies now) for this work. But there is something beyond me, something outside of me, which impels me irresistibly."[3]

There was nothing mystical about this. Robert Peary loved the immensity of the forces against which he pitted himself. He loved the elemental simplicity of life in the Far North. "Wonderful this cabin, this mellow light . . . this freedom from care or annoyance, this freedom to do as I please." He had always loved this freedom as a boy and young man, even though he also wanted to be part of society. In the Arctic he could shed this social side. Despite Bridgman's urging, despite his mutilated feet, despite his genuine love for Jo, he would not go back.

Winter came once again, and once more they moved supplies to Fort Conger by moonlight, but this time in two stages. They went north on the Greenland side and waited there over the two weeks of moonless nights. When the moon returned once again, they crossed the sea ice to Cape Sabine on

Ellesmere Island and went north to Fort Conger. They were delighted to find a herd of musk oxen nearby; there would be no danger of starvation for the Peary party as there had been for Greely's. Since musk oxen grazed in the same areas for years, Peary found it impossible to understand why Greely's men could not have sustained themselves by hunting until rescue parties arrived. He was critical of Greely, and later made his criticisms known and made another enemy.

In April 1900 Peary decided the time was once again ripe to try for the Pole, but this time he decided to go via northern Greenland. Should the Pole elude him again, at least he would have mapped that part of Greenland and perhaps been the first to stand at Greenland's most northern edge. Henson and five Eskimos accompanied Peary, each with a sledge. One of the Eskimos fell ill almost immediately. It was Ahngoodloo, who had so carefully handled the sledge after Peary's toes were amputated. Now it was Peary's turn. He took Ahngoodloo back to Fort Conger, then hastened to catch up with Henson and the others in Greenland.

They reached Cape Washington, which had been seen but not explored by Lieutenant J. B. Lockwood and Sergeant D. W. Brainard, two members of Greely's party who had been sent to Greenland. It was thought possible that Cape Washington was the top of Greenland. To Bert's satisfaction, there was still more land to the north, and he could still be the man to stand at the top of Greenland, and thus at the top of the world's land mass, for the first time. Five days later, Peary fulfilled his wish when he and his men reached the land, a cape that Peary named after his friend and sponsor, Morris K. Jesup. (In the late 1980s, geographers using sophisticated measuring instruments determined that the tiny island of Oodaaq off Cape Morris K. Jesup was the north-ernmost point of land in the world.)

The men went out on the ocean ice for three marches in a rather halfhearted attempt to reach the Pole. Fog, rafting ice, the smoky "water sky" that always meant open water below, and the in-creasing pain in Peary's still-tender stumps, forced them back. He was not really ready for traveling far over ocean ice. The group traveled eastward instead, naming another cape after Herbert L. Bridgman. They sighted the other side of Mount Wistar, which Peary had discovered in 1895, and knew that they had covered virtually all of the top of Greenland and established it definitely as an island. It was with a certain amount of satisfaction that this Peary expe-dition ended, returning to Fort Conger in June.

Peary decided that they would stay in Fort Con-ger instead of going on to Etah—an unlucky and unhappy decision, for Josephine and little Marie Ahnighito were on their way to a surprise reunion with Bert. When they reached Etah, the Eskimos told Jo they thought Peary was at Cape Sabine, and the *Windward* worked its way there. Winds drove the ship onto the rocks, and fearing she might break up, everyone went over the side onto land. But the ship stayed in one piece, and everyone got back on board to sit out the winter until the ice broke up and the ship could be refloated. Those on the *Windward* realized by now that Peary was in Fort Conger, but no one would chance taking a mes-sage to him until spring. So there they sat, Bert and Jo, at either end of Kane Basin, so close but so far apart.

Jo made an unfortunate discovery while waiting on the ship. She had come to bring solace to her husband, but she found out he didn't really need any. Allakasingwah was among the Eskimos on board, and as the two women whiled away the time in idle talk, she innocently bragged about her relationship with Peary, not understanding that it was not news Jo would welcome. Jo took the blow quietly. Lacking any means of immediate communication with her husband, she sat down that evening and wrote him a letter that he would not read until they saw each other again. The letter was almost an apology: "You will have been surprised, perhaps annoyed, when you hear that I came up on a ship . . . but believe me had I known how things were with you here I should not have come."[4]

Jo and Allakasingwah, whom Jo called Allie, mourned together over Bert's amputations, and when Allakasingwah took ill and it seemed as if she might die, Jo helped her. She was concerned, too, that Allakasingwah's—and Bert's—baby would be killed if the young Eskimo woman died. Until a child reached two years of age, he or she was constantly carried by the mother in the hood of her anorak. It was the custom to strangle a child still "in the hood" when the mother died. Jo made the Eskimos promise not to kill this baby should Allakasingwah die. She never found out whether they would have kept the promise, because Allie lived. (She would have another of Bert's sons in 1906.)

The strange winter passed slowly, with Bert in Fort Conger, Jo chafing at Cape Sabine, and little Marie Ahnighito having a wonderful time playing with the Eskimo children and learning to speak the Polar Eskimo language. Since Eskimo children are never disciplined and eat and sleep as they please, this situation must have created some interesting problems for Jo. But they all thrived, even in the long winter darkness aboard the icebound ship.

The same could not be said for those at Fort Conger. Perhaps it was the place, the isolation, or too

80

Crew of the *Erik* on a stopover in Upernavik,
then the northernmost trading center in Greenland.
These Eskimo girls and women dress quite differently
from their counterparts farther north. The bead embroidery
(far right) is typical and shows European influence.

This ice crush cost the *Roosevelt* a rudder, stern post, and part of a propeller.

No problem crossing this small lead .

Storm Camp: jammed up at the Big Lead

Eskimo drawings made while waiting at Storm Camp to cross the Big Lead. These Eskimos had never seen paper and pencils before Peary reached them, yet they display great talent.

Peary enjoys a rare moment of fatherhood as he waits
to go exploring once more. This is a different kind of "sledge"
(note runners) than he is accustomed to!

President Theodore Roosevelt bidding Peary bon voyage
at Oyster Bay

Captain Bob Bartlett and Donald MacMillan aboard the *Roosevelt*

The deck of the *Roosevelt*.
This photo was taken by Matthew Henson.

Bringing water back to the ship is no easy matter.
This precarious perch is the end of the line
for members of the bucket brigade.

Had it been visible, the onset of the successful expedition
to the Pole would have looked just like this start
of a previous journey.

Waiting to start on the race to the Pole, Peary and friends take time to pose

Ross Marvin, whose mysterious death cast the first long
shadow on the Peary Expedition's victory in achieving the Pole

Matthew Henson, after the achievement of the Pole

Lunch on the run. The Peary stove provides a little warmth
and hot tea at the same time.

Celebrating the discovery of the Pole.
Left to right: Ooqueah and the Navy League flag;
Ootah and the Delta Kappa Epsilon (Peary's fraternity) flag;
Henson with the flag Josephine Peary made for this moment;
Egingwah with the Daughters of the American Revolution
peace flag; and Seegloo with the flag of the Red Cross.
Peary took the picture, and admitted
that while some of the flags seemed incongruous,
they brightened this momentous occasion.

Peary's famous announcement of having reached the Pole

Cook (on the right) at a reception in his honor after claiming
he had reached the Pole. Mrs. Cook is behind him.

long a time spent in the Arctic. The Eskimos seemed to be all right, but something was happening to Peary and the other men, particularly Dedrick. Peary annoyed Dedrick; Dedrick annoyed Peary. Henson annoyed Dedrick; the Eskimos annoyed Dedrick. The Eskimos liked to say that Peary was the middle finger (the longest), Henson the ring finger, and Dedrick—they laughed as they said this—was the little finger. Dedrick saw this as a terrible insult. He did not realize that he had often insulted the Eskimos, particularly by refusing to enter into sexual relations with the women, and they were getting back at him. That Henson should be more important to Peary, that Dedrick should have to cook for a black man when it was his turn at kitchen duty—these were intolerable things to Dedrick. He took to cooking for himself, and sometimes Bert joined him to keep the peace. But Dedrick's appearance—he had stopped shaving and cutting his hair—and his increasingly erratic behavior alarmed Peary.

Dedrick demanded that Henson be given written instructions about proper deportment. Peary did not do this, but he did speak to Henson, who, he thought, was not showing him respect. Peary jotted down notes for this talk:

> Intend start in this winter with every possible source of annoyance, irritation, or misunderstanding removed.
> Have cleared up some matters with doctor. Now it's your turn, then the Eskimos. . . .
> Not only reality but even appearance or suspicion of unfairness to be avoided. . . .
> Must come to me about everything, no matter how small, for use or consumption.
> Am old enough now and you have been in my

service long enough to show me respect in small things.

Have a right to expect you will say sir to me always. That you will pay attention when I am talking to you and show that you hear directions I give you by saying yes sir, or all right sir.

Have no fault to find when we are alone together, but when doctor or number of Eskimos present or we are on board ship you are very different. . . .

Now is there anything which, if different, would make things pleasanter for you?[5]

It was the naval lieutenant talking to the lower ranks. The results are unknown, although we do know that in later years whenever Henson wrote to Peary, he always addressed him as "Dear Sir."

Dedrick continued his erratic behavior to the point of wanting to go to the Pole by himself when Henson and Peary showed signs of ill health. Peary had had enough by now, and under the weather or not, they would stop sitting around going mad and start out for the Pole. He planned for Henson and one Eskimo to accompany him the whole way, while Dedrick would turn back after one march and take charge at Fort Conger. That was the last straw for Dedrick, who presented his resignation. He immediately regretted the decision—Fort Conger was not exactly the place for a gesture of this sort—and retracted his resignation.

After only eight days on the sea ice, Henson and Peary had to turn back. They really were in no shape to face this. A few days after their return, runners from the *Windward* came searching for them with the news that Jo and Marie Ahnighito were waiting aboard ship. After a brief rest, Peary sledged down Kane Basin, reaching Cape Sabine and Jo on his forty-fifth birthday, May 6, 1901.

Jo and Bert finally had several months together. Then it was summer and the relief ship, the *Erik*, arrived. It brought a new expedition member, Charles Percy, a steward and superb cook. And the *Erik* also brought news that Mary Wiley Peary had died on November 4, 1900, convinced that her son had died before her. She had seen so little of him, and their letters to and from the Arctic often took a year or more to be delivered. Peary's grief immobilized him. How many letters had he written to her after she was dead, never guessing she was gone? Here are parts of one, written on April 4, 1901, five months to the day after she died:

Hardly an hour, certainly not a day, has passed that I have not longed for you, and Jo, and my babies. I have been . . . very, very selfish, and yet I know that you have forgiven me, for you have been with me so many times, and averted trouble [for] me. In my journey of last spring, things happened in which I know you took a part, and yet they seem so strange that were another person telling me of them, I should be incredulous. . . . In three instances bears passed close to caches of food which I had made for our return, caches which were very important if not vital to our return, without disturbing them. Another time a bear walked over a cache, yet let it alone. Once, open water which barred my passage froze over to let me pass, and twelve hours later was open water again. Repeatedly I had the most vivid dreams of you. I know you are watching over me. I am not sick, mother, not worried nor discouraged. But I am older and I see many things more clearly. God bless and keep you.[6]

It was good that Jo and Marie were there for him, and he watched them leave on the *Windward* at the end of August with more sadness in his heart. He didn't have much time to brood about them, however, for another crisis arose. The *Erik* was supposed to take Dr. Dedrick back. He had resigned again, a decision Peary found most acceptable in view of the doctor's increasingly strange behavior. But now Dedrick refused to board the ship. Instead, he set up a campsite and plagued Peary by continually dropping in on him, declaiming on various subjects until he fell into a babble. It was obvious that the man was mentally ill, a cause for considerable fear among the Eskimos. Even when an epidemic of a dysentery-like disease ran rampant among the Eskimos, killing six of them, Peary did not call on Dedrick for assistance. He nursed them himself with Henson's help. After that, Peary had no communication at all with Dedrick, who finally left Greenland at some unknown date, probably aboard a whaler.

In the spring following this tumultuous time, Peary, Henson, and four Eskimos attempted a journey on foot on to the Arctic Ocean from Payer Harbor. Once again they were thwarted by rafted ice so high they could hardly climb it and by young ice so soft it would not support a sledge. Temperatures reached $-60°F.$, so that their breath froze on their faces, and the wind was so bitter and icy it felt like knives slashing their eyes. And once again they turned back, but not before establishing a new farthest-north record.

Then it was August, and the *Windward* was back with Jo and Marie to take the Peary expedition home.

C H A P T E R

VI

GREAT EXPLORATIONS, UNMET EXPECTATIONS

There were more gold medals—from the Société de Géographie in France and the Royal Scottish Geographical Society—and more fame for Peary when he arrived home. In 1903 he was elected to the presidency of the American Geographical Society, a position the Navy allowed him to accept. He also passed Navy examinations for promotion to lieutenant commander and then commander. On the personal side, he and Jo had a son, Robert Jr., on August 29, 1903.

Peary was actually working at being in the Navy for a change, and his assignment was a good one—he was sent to Great Britain to study the construction of naval barracks. Back in Washington he lobbied for a reorganization of the Civil Engineers Corps. But to him, these activities were bypaths.

Peary had undergone another operation in which his little toes were amputated so they wouldn't get in the way. This allowed the doctors to draw the skin together in a protective cushion over the stumps. Peary's gait was better, although it was still more a glide than a step, and he had less pain. He was ready to try for the Pole again.

Peary's plea to win the Pole for the United States sounded good to the new man in the White House, Theodore Roosevelt. He had followed Peary's efforts in the Arctic and admired him. The two men were very similar in their love of adventure and nature, their self-reliance and individualism. Both, too, were strongly patriotic. The United States was beginning to take its place among the world powers, and winning the Pole would enhance that position. Teddy Roosevelt saw to it that Peary was given the official backing of the United States government for the first time. There would be no more fighting for leave from the Navy, but funding for the expedition would still have to come from private sources. Again, the members of the Peary Arctic Club opened their wallets, and Morris K. Jesup added something extra. Bert again had to come up with matching funds raised by lectures, the writing of books and articles by both the Pearys, and donations.

The ship for this expedition would be very special, capable of getting through the ice to a higher latitude than Peary's ships had achieved before. In this way, the walk to the Pole would be as short as possible. The ship was designed and its construction supervised by Peary. It was made of wood for easy repair and better resistance to the sharp edges of icebergs. (Ten years later, the great steel hull of the *Titanic* would be cut open by an iceberg as if it were a can of tuna.) The inside of Peary's ship was reinforced with steel, and it was powered by steam engines and auxiliary sails. Peary, still the engineer, devised a way for the engines to put on a double surge of power to move out of the ice when necessary, and the propeller and shaft were oversize to accommodate the greater power. The hull was egg-shaped, to help the ship move out of the squeezing action of the pack ice. On the deck were winches and windlasses and steam capstans for hauling the ship out of the ice or off the rocks, and hanging over the sides were six whaleboats for short trips and emergencies. The ship was christened the *Roosevelt* by Jo's breaking a champagne bottle across her bow.

The expedition got under way on July 16, 1905, the *Erik* following the *Roosevelt* with supplies. The *Roosevelt*'s captain was Robert A. Bartlett, a Newfoundlander whom Peary had met and liked when Bartlett was a mate aboard the *Windward* years before. There were two other old hands aboard: Matt Henson and the steward Charles Percy. The two new men were Dr. Louis G. Wolf, a young surgeon, and Ross G. Marvin of Cornell University, who was to act as assistant and expedition secretary.

The voyage went well despite some trouble with the boilers, and they were soon at Etah. This time, however, Peary was not going to use Etah and Fort Conger as bases. Instead they would sail the *Roosevelt* as far north as they could, anchor it in the ice, and stay aboard. They transferred supplies from the *Erik*, picked up over fifty Eskimo men, women, and children and two hundred dogs, and were on their way through ice that few ships had ever been able to break; only four other ships had made it up the channel, and only three had made it back. As they passed Fort Conger, ice damaged the rudder, but they were able to make temporary repairs. Three weeks after they had started out, they were at their new home: Cape Sheridan, at the top of Grant Land on the Lincoln Sea. Lying at anchor, the ship rode out several life-threatening attacks by icebergs and huge cakes of rafting sea ice that "shivered her timbers" and made her thrum like guitar strings. Soon the colder weather prevented such attacks—everything was frozen in place and nothing could move.

The expedition's home was not so desolate as it may sound. Peary's cabin had a small library of books, a Pianola player piano that played rolls of music automatically, and a Victrola to play records. The party ate well. Charles Percy provided two meals a day: cereal and eggs with sausage or ham might make breakfast; corned beef, musk ox steak with canned vegetables, bread and butter, dessert, and tea made a satisfying dinner. Peary particularly enjoyed the musk ox, as did the Eskimos, although he ate his cooked and the Eskimos barely warmed theirs. Whale meat was another dish favored by both the Eskimos and their dogs, but when eight of the dogs died from what proved to be poisoned whale meat, several tons of it had to be scrapped and more musk oxen hunted.

Toward the end of February 1906 there was enough light for the trip to the Pole to begin. The men were to work something like a bucket brigade moving water to a fire. A team of several Eskimos headed by an expedition member would move onto the Arctic Ocean ice, to be followed a day or so later by still another team, then another. When the second team caught up with the first team, waiting about fifty miles ahead, it would pick up supplies and go forward some distance and wait for the third team to arrive and take the supplies. It then would go back to pick up more supplies from the first team, which had gone back to the base to get them. This would go on for as many teams as Peary put together, and the last team would be freshest and fastest, having gone most of the distance without hauling supplies. Teams would not always wait, but might cache the supplies, and, of course, each team used some of the supplies for the trips out and back.

When it worked, this system worked well. It didn't usually work, however. Spacing collapsed when difficulties slowed the parties down. The difficulties were many: the pressure ridges, where huge floes of ice rafted crazily against the shore and each other and backed up for miles; the rough hummocks of ice; the leads, areas of open water in the sea ice; the broken sledges; the trail of the forward party lost in a storm, or on moving ice, or in an opening lead. . . .

Peary fashioned four teams for this trek. They made it over the pressure ridges, but shortly afterward piled up at a wide lead that at one time or another he would call the Big Lead, the Hudson River, and the River Styx. (Peary was to conclude, and he was confirmed in his conclusion, that this Big Lead marked the continental shelf, the underwater border of the North American continent at about latitude 84° north.) The expedition members could wait there until it froze over so they could cross, or they could turn around and go home. Peary chose to wait—and wait—and wait. The teams waited six days at the Big Lead until they could finally cross, but by then their food supplies were depleted. Peary abandoned plans for a stretched-out supply line in favor of sharing resources and moving on together. A violent blizzard held them back for six more days, huddled in a cluster of snow igloos that they named, appropriately, Storm Camp.

Observations showed that the ice they were on was drifting eastward, moved by winds and currents in the ocean below. If they didn't move faster, they would find themselves having to make a much longer return journey because they would end up in Greenland, far to the east of the *Roosevelt*. They might not have enough supplies for such a long journey. They might even drift so far east that they would miss Greenland altogether and never get back to land. Speed was vital, and Peary decided to take Henson and make a dash for the Pole. But they soon found themselves tiring, the dogs were giving out, and there were too many leads to cross and too few supplies. They were defeated. Still, they had reached latitude 87°6' north, farther north than anyone had ever before traveled. They were only a bit more than two degrees from the Pole. Peary raised the flags he had been keeping for the Pole, buried a bottle containing a record of the trip and a piece of the guidon Jo had made for his first Christmas in the Arctic, and they turned back.

The men met up with only two of the three support groups, and once again at the 84th parallel they encountered the Big Lead, now half a mile wide. A lead cutting them off from home on the return journey would be fatal—they couldn't go forward, and they needn't go back. This was when Peary changed the name of the Big Lead to the Styx, the mythical river over which the souls of the dead are said to be ferried.

The next day Peary scouted about and found an area of new ice formation that might allow them to cross the lead. As they started across, this ice bridge began to give way. They scrambled back onto shore just in time and watched as more leads opened all around them, cutting them off. Each day a dog or two had to be shot for food and was cooked over fires made from broken sledges. And each day scouts would search for a way to cross the Big Lead, now about two miles wide. Finally two Eskimos came hurrying into the camp with the news that "young ice"—newly formed—had bridged the lead. If they moved quickly and skimmed over the surface lightly on snowshoes, they had a good chance. Peary would write about this crossing:

When we started it was with Panikpah, lightest of us all and most experienced in the lead, the few remaining dogs attached to the long broad-runner sledge. We crossed in silence, each man busy with his thoughts and intent upon his snowshoes. . . . Once started, we could not stop; we could not lift our snowshoes. It was a matter of constantly and smoothly gliding one past the other with utmost care and evenness of pressure, and from every man as he slid a snowshoe forward, undulations went out in every direction through the thin film incrusting the black water. The sledge was preceded and followed by a broad swell.

It was the first and only time in all my Arctic work that I felt doubtful as to the outcome, but when near the middle of the lead the toe of my rear kamik . . . broke through twice in succession, I thought to myself "This is the finish," and when a little later there was a cry from someone in the line, the words sprang from me of themselves, "God help him; which one is it?" But I dared not take my eyes from the steady, even gliding of my snowshoes, and the fascination of the glassy swell at the toes of them.

. . . We stepped upon the firm ice on the southern side of the lead. . . . The sighs of relief . . . [were] distinctly audible. . . . The cry I had heard had been from one of my men whose toe, like mine, had broken through the ice. . . . We looked back [and] the lead was widening again and we had just made it.[1]

Now the men faced "such a hell of shattered ice as I had never seen before . . . from the size of paving stones to literally and without exaggeration the dome of the Capitol. . . . It did not seem as if anything not possessing wings could negotiate it." But somehow they did, falling frequently, which for Peary was particularly painful because of his tender stumps. Finally they were on land—Greenland.

Almost miraculously, they met up with their fourth team, led by Charles Clark, a fireman on the *Roosevelt* who had been recruited for the ice journey. He and the three Eskimos in his team had run out of food and had been eating their spare kamiks for whatever nourishment the skin boots could give. They were close to death from starvation. The others did what they could, but there was little to give. Then Peary recognized the mountains of Peary Land in the distance and knew they were not far from musk oxen. Once again the meat saved their lives. Restored, the men struck out for the *Roosevelt,* reaching it in early May.

Never one to be still for long, Peary and a few others were off again in a few weeks to explore Grant Land and Axel Heiberg Island to the west. At the northwest tip, which he named Cape Thomas Hubbard, Peary, searching the horizon through his binoculars, saw what he thought was a land formation off to the northwest. He named this Crocker Land and envied the man who would one day explore it. He would soon meet the man, Donald B. MacMillan, who would accompany Peary on his next and last expedition. MacMillan was also to see Crocker Land, but he could never step on it, for it didn't exist. It was a mirage, an optical phenomenon, a trick of air and reflected light that occurs frequently over Arctic waters. Many Arctic travelers have been completely taken in by the mirages, and Peary was one. (Sir John Ross of the "Iron Mountain" was another: he insisted that land blocked his ships' passage and turned back a major expedition, for which he was disgraced.) It should have been a matter of no consequence, but "Crocker Land," which found its way onto maps of the period, would later be used to try to prove Peary "unreliable."

The trip back to the *Roosevelt* in the warm July weather was a struggle against thawing ice—a kind of white mud—and pools of meltwater. The party finally reached Grant Land, where they met up with Ross Marvin and a party taking soundings—depth measurements of the waters. Marvin told them that the *Roosevelt* had been able to free itself from the ice and had moved south from Cape Sheridan, but was stuck fast once again after losing a propeller and the rudder.

The tired men finally caught up with the ship, where Peary spent the next three weeks worrying: Would the ice retreat and let them go so they would not have to winter over another year? Could the rudder and propeller be repaired? Could they find enough wood to burn, now that their coal supply was exhausted? The answer to all three questions proved to be yes, and they were soon homeward bound.

Perhaps Peary had a moment when he felt less contemptuous of Greely, when he appreciated the role of luck in exploring the Arctic, for luck had played its part in getting the Peary expedition home safely. We do know he was humbled by the experience. He wrote, "To think . . . what a little journey it is on the map and how far short of my hopes it fell. To think that I have failed once more, that I shall never have a chance to win again."[2] But he did.

C H A P T E R

VII

THE
BRASS RING

Delays—time passing—others will get there first.

Delays—time passing—he was growing older. Too old.

Delays, delays, delays—this refitting of the *Roosevelt* would never be finished, people were dunning him for money in a very ungentlemanly fashion, and somehow they would have to be paid.

Robert Peary's impatience was consuming him. He wanted to be off again; it was all he could think of. He had written the book and the articles and given all the lectures to raise the money he needed to match the Peary Arctic Club's financing. People across the nation had sent him small amounts of their hard-earned money to help. Then Morris Jesup had suddenly died. Added to Peary's sorrow at losing a friend was his despair at not getting the money Jesup personally had pledged. Mrs. Jesup had not forgotten her husband's pledge, however, and she sent the expedition a large contribution. General Thomas H. Hubbard, the new president of the Peary Arctic Club, added to his original contribution. But there still wasn't enough money.

Then, miraculously, the money was there. Zenas Crane, the paper magnate, unexpectedly donated so generously that the expedition was, at last, fully financed. "What this $10,000 meant to me at that time would need the pen of Shakespeare to make entirely clear," Peary was to write.

Teddy Roosevelt had arranged for Peary to remain on active duty for this trip so that there would be no more half-pay leave to worry about. He was attached to the U.S. Coast and Geodetic Survey and ordered to chart the waters around Grant Land and northern Greenland. Peary had put together a strong and larger team of men this time: Matt Henson; Ross Marvin and Captain Bob Bartlett from the 1905–06 expedition; Donald B. MacMillan, a teacher and fellow Bowdoin alumnus; Dr. J. W. Goodsell; and George Borup, an eager, brand-new Yale graduate. Fifteen more men were hired to crew the *Roosevelt*.

They finally weighed anchor on July 6, 1908. The crowds cheered, the ships in the harbor blasted their horns in salute, the sun was bright brass, the water silver and undulating foam. Dozens of flags brightened the dreary waterfront as they sailed slowly up New York's East River toward Long Island Sound and the Oyster Bay home of President Roosevelt. Here they would be given the honor of a presidential tour of inspection; then Jo and Bert would return to New York City on a tug while their two children, in the care of a friend and "the boys," would sail on to Sydney, Nova Scotia. Bert and Jo would travel by train to Sydney to meet the ship and her passengers when she docked.

At Sydney, the *Roosevelt* took on coal and tons of whale meat, and final good-byes were said. In mid-July, the men were off for Greenland. The first stop was Cape York, where they bartered for dogs and furs and picked up a few Eskimo families. Farther up the coast, the *Erik*, with several paying passengers aboard for the summer, was waiting. Peary and Henson transferred to her to sail along the coast recruiting Eskimos and finding dogs while the *Roosevelt* went on to Etah, where she would be cleaned and made ready for the battle with the ice. Peary hoped the *Roosevelt* would be able to work her way through the ice to a point beyond the Big Lead, saving the men from having to cross that River Styx with sledges. Otherwise, Peary had explained in a statement published before they sailed, the expedition would follow the same main features as the previous one, except that the parties would keep closer together so as not to get separated and that the route would compensate more for the eastward drift of the ice.

The *Erik* and its passengers sailed on to meet the *Roosevelt* at Etah. One of the passengers, a Harry Whitney, asked Peary's permission to stay at the settlement until the following year. Peary intended to station two men to guard the fifty tons of coal and the whale meat he would be leaving at Etah in preparation for their return. He felt Whitney would have sufficient protection there and allowed him to stay on.

At Etah, a half-crazed white man wanted just as badly to leave. He came running at them, babbling about having to get away and waving a letter from Dr. Frederick A. Cook, with whom he had arrived the previous year. His name was Rudolph Franke, and he had not been able or willing to go on with Cook. In the letter, written the previous year, Cook gave permission for Franke to leave. But giving permission and providing the means are not the same thing. Franke, having spent a year at Etah with no sign of a ship and unable or unwilling to eat Eskimo fare that would have prevented the scurvy from which he was suffering, thought he had been marooned forever.

Franke told Peary that Cook might be trying for the Pole. Peary could not believe that. Cook had taken only two Eskimos with him. Three men could not possibly manage enough sledges to carry supplies for such a long expedition. Cook also had no experience with sea ice. In fact, Cook's only other forays into the Arctic had been with Peary on the first crossing of the ice cap, and he had not ventured far onto the ice then, and as the conductor of a botched tourist expedition to Greenland. (In 1894 Cook had brought seventy-five paying passengers on a small ship he had chartered—and did not insure—that had been wrecked on landing. Cook and a few men had taken a small boat south to find a ship to bring them home again, and all the others had to fend for themselves in an Eskimo village too small to support such a huge influx of people. The ship's provisions were completely inadequate: Cook had turned the matter of buying supplies over to a recent college graduate who had no idea of what was needed for such an expedition. A whaling ship that was willing to lose a year's income in order to return the Cook group to civilization was finally found and its master and crew given a promissory note for compensation. But the note remained unpaid for several years. Cook could or would not use any part of the money he had received in fares, and the members of the group finally resorted to writing books and giving benefit dinners to raise money to compensate their rescuers.) Cook had had some

98

experience in the Antarctic, where he went as a surgeon with an expedition, but Antarctic travel is over land ice, not sea ice.

Peary dismissed Cook from his mind. But he had also been told long before that Cook might fake the discovery. Dr. Cook had apparently faked the first ascent to the top of Mount McKinley in Alaska. He had been on a failed expedition to climb the mountain, and after the other climbers had left, he claimed to have reached the summit by himself. He presented as evidence photographs later proven to be faked. That had not stopped some people from believing him. That Cook might fake the achievement of the Pole was not unlikely. But Peary hadn't entertained the possibility for one second. "Dr. Cook is a gentleman," he said, and that took care of that. Peary had even written a letter, dated April 12, 1908, before he left for Greenland, that stated, "if the burden of bringing Cook back rests on Mrs. Cook's shoulders, I shall be willing to waive all personal feelings out of consideration for her difficult position and recommend to the [Peary Arctic] Club that [he] be brought back for a nominal sum, on the . . . [Erik], which goes north this summer."[1]

Peary was probably not too enthusiastic about fulfilling that promise now, but it would be a year before the situation needed to be faced. Reasoning that Cook was off exploring Ellesmere Island, Peary gave written instructions to the two men he was leaving behind to guard Cook's supplies and equipment as well as their own and to give Cook whatever help he needed when he returned. Franke was to go back on the Erik—for a fee. Peary was annoyed at the whole affair and impatient to be off. He had chosen twenty-two of the best Eskimo men and seventeen women with ten children, and he had acquired 264 dogs. It was time to go.

The passage to Cape Sheridan was crowded with icebergs and ice floes pushing hither and thither on tides from Baffin Bay in the south and the Lincoln Sea in the north. Often extending 80 to 100 feet above water, and seven times that below, the bergs loomed higher than the ship. Now hoping that the bergs would not crash into them or tumble and swamp them, now eluding the surge of ice on the tides by dodging into a sheltered cove, now hoping not to be squeezed between the ice and the rocks, they worked their way slowly north. Peary knew every foot of the coastline, and Captain Bob, as Bartlett was called, knew all about ships in ice. Together they did a magnificent job of navigating through all the hazards. Just the same, the ship's six small whaleboats were filled with food and readied for use in case the *Roosevelt* had to be abandoned. All on board kept a bundle of essentials with them at all times to take into the boats at a moment's notice, and they didn't take their clothes off at any time.

This kind of traveling was slow going, and the new "boys" took language lessons from the Eskimos with Henson, an expert, translating. They went over the side of the ship to hunt now and then or, like Peary, just to get away from the people and the dogs and the formidable smell of both.

Shifting, backing, charging, skirting, the *Roosevelt* inched its way north. On August 29, Peary, Henson, and Charles Percy drank a bottle of champagne in honor of the fifth birthday of Bertie, Jr. The day after the party, the water was so turbulent that a huge mass of moving sea ice attacked the shore, where, unfortunately, the ship was tied up to a beached iceberg. Now the berg was in the air, and then, in response to the laws of gravity, its tons of ice came smashing down—right through Ross Marvin's cabin. One of the lines tangled the propeller, and only split-second work untangled it in time to prevent serious damage. Then another iceberg suddenly split as if it had been struck by lightning, and a chunk of ice the size of a very large living room shot by like a missile and missed crushing the ship by only a foot or two. To save the reeling ship, Peary decided to use dynamite to break up all the surrounding ice into smaller pieces that could not do so much damage. The tactic worked, but now the ice battered the ship and rolled it from one side to the other.

Finally a lead widened, allowing the *Roosevelt* to get out of there. It was one of the few times Peary was glad to see a widening lead, but a widening lead when you are on foot and when you are on a ship are two different things. In the first instance, it can mean death; in the second, life. Moving up the lead under a full head of steam, they finally reached Cape Sheridan. They were supposed to go twenty-five miles farther, but after only two miles they saw another ice barrier looming ahead, and Peary decided Cape Sheridan would have to do. But those two miles gave the *Roosevelt* the honor of sailing farther north than any other vessel under its own steam. (The *Fram*, Fridtjof Nansen's ship, had achieved a higher latitude, but it was not under its own power. It had been deliberately allowed to get frozen into the ice to see if the currents would take it over the Pole, which they did not, although they did take the ship over the top of the world.)

At Cape Sheridan, supplies and equipment were unloaded. Packing boxes were converted into huts to use as workplaces or as shelters should the ship meet with a mishap. Provisions were stacked high, and the huts and the ship were ready to face the long winter. Hunting parties went out but were

101

none too successful. This led Peary to fear that the game had gone elsewhere after being hunted on the previous visit. The women went out with traps and fishing gear (fishing was considered too lowly a job for Eskimo men who were fit enough to hunt) and did bring in Arctic foxes and a huge number of fish.

MacMillan, Marvin, and Borup took tidal observations for the Coast and Geodetic Survey. Sledges began to transport supplies to Cape Columbia to the west and some miles north—another maneuver to make the walk to the Pole shorter. The sledging trips had the added value of breaking in the new men. These members of the expedition had to learn many essential things. They had to find out how to wear and care for their new fur clothing, how to keep the heavy sledges upright, how to control the virtually uncontrollable Eskimo dogs, how to deal with frosted noses, ears, and toes, and how to keep their Eskimo assistants happy. They also needed to know how to get in and out of a snow igloo, how to sleep in a small canvas tent, or *tupik,* in their furs on a musk ox fur mattress and under a caribou blanket, how to stay asleep when the Eskimos chanted their songs at whatever hour pleased them, and what to do when alcohol stoves used up all the air. They learned to share a single teaspoon among five or six men—Peary regarded utensils as extra weight—and to use a hunting knife to spear meat from a pot made out of the bottom of a five-gallon can. A second such pot was kept for boiling water for tea, a beverage Peary considered indispensable for warming the body and comforting the soul.

Charles Percy's meals aboard the *Roosevelt* were also comforting and certainly more elegant both in content and in service. Water was obtained from ponds or melted from icebergs if they needed it badly enough to use precious fuel for the process. A good pond was preferable and treated with care. To keep the pond from freezing, the men would cover it with a wooden trapdoor over which they would build a snow igloo.

Lights went out at midnight, with small allowances made for particular needs or desires. The Eskimos were accustomed to sleeping and eating as they pleased, but they were asked to respect the ship's routine and generally complied. Otherwise, a polite reminder would go out that they not sing or dance or make loud noises between 10:00 P.M. and 8:00 A.M.

Peary spent the winter on board the ship, writing, working on his design for what he called the Peary sledge (lighter and longer than the Eskimo sledges), instructing the women on details he wanted in the clothing they were making, experimenting with a new alcohol stove he had designed, and calculating the weight of everything going on the sledges so that they would pull only the essential minimum amount.

One night in November, the ice, which had been quiet for weeks, suddenly menaced the ship, pushing it toward land on a surging tide. The *Roosevelt* started to keel over, and everyone raced to put out all the lamps and stoves to prevent a fire—a dreaded disaster in the Arctic, where there is little or no water to douse the flames. The danger was over in five or six hours as the tide receded and the ice action stopped, but the *Roosevelt* was frozen at an uncomfortable, disorienting angle until spring.

Another worry for the party was the deteriorating health of the dogs. By the end of November, only 160 of the 264 dogs they had brought with them were still alive. Without enough dogs there could be no expedition. Peary and the men tried different foods, but not until an extra cache of wal-

103

rus meat was found and fed to them did the dogs come around. Walrus meat helped prevent scurvy in the Eskimos, and the dogs may have been suffering from a vitamin deficiency disease like scurvy that responded to the vitamin C in the meat.

Finally the last moon of winter did its two-week turn, and the sledge teams moved on to Cape Columbia in the spring twilight to make their trek to the Pole—413 miles of racing over a moving, cracking cover of ice that averaged ten feet thick on an ocean thousands of feet deep. There would be the rafting ice, where the pack ice crashed into the shore or into the edges of leads and piled up the ice coming behind it. There would be the leads, where the cracking ice opened and let the water come to the surface—and that surface might be under an igloo. There would be the hummocks, the hills of rough ice sometimes twenty feet high. As Peary described it:

> The difficulties and hardships of a journey to the North Pole are too complex to be summed up in a paragraph. But, briefly stated, the worst of them are: the ragged and mountainous ice over which the traveler must journey with his heavily loaded sledges; the often terrific wind, having the impact of a wall of water, which he must march against at times; the open leads . . . he must cross and recross, somehow; the intense cold . . . through which he must—by fur clothing and constant activity—keep his flesh from freezing; the difficulty of dragging out and back of the ragged and "lead"-interrupted trail enough pemmican, biscuit, tea, condensed milk, and liquid fuel to keep sufficient strength in the body for traveling. It was so cold much of the time . . . that the brandy was frozen solid, the petroleum was white and viscid, and the dogs could hardly be seen for the steam of their

breath. . . . At times one may be obliged to march all day long facing a blinding snowstorm with the bitter wind searching every opening in the clothing. . . . Imagine tramping through such a storm all day long, over jagged and uneven ice, with the temperature between fifteen and thirty degrees below zero, and no shelter to look forward to at the end of the day's march excepting a narrow and cold snow house which they would themselves be obliged to build in that very storm before they could eat or rest.[2]

Peary, Henson, Bartlett, MacMillan, Marvin, Borup, Dr. Goodsell, and fourteen Eskimos formed seven teams, with 133 dogs and nineteen sledges. Twenty-four-hour daylight would soon be upon them. The weather had been clear and calm up to the day they left, March 1, but then high winds stirred up so much snow that the usual sounds of an expedition—dogs snarling and barking, driver shouting—were completely muffled, an eerie and somewhat somber beginning. With Bartlett pioneering the trail, they moved out onto the sea, crossing the "crazy" ice, as Peary called the rafting ice, with great difficulty. It was easier going after that, but the surface was uneven and hard on the sledges—wood gets brittle at −50°F.—and some of the parties had to stop to make repairs before they even reached the first camp Bartlett had set up for them.

On the first day they were plagued by other problems as well. Peary's leg, broken so many years before, suddenly started bothering him. Before he could rest at the end of the march, one of the Eskimos on Henson's team came wiggling through the tunnel that opened into Peary's snow igloo, calling out that *Tornarsuk* the devil was in camp and was keeping them from lighting their stove. Peary went over and discovered that the severe cold kept the alcohol in his newly designed stove from vaporizing. The vapor had to be ignited to flame the alcohol. Using a piece of paper all the men carried to keep notes on, Peary fashioned a wick, and *Tornarsuk* disappeared. Up ahead Bartlett and Borup had solved the same problem by heating the alcohol. The solutions were fortunate, for without workable stoves the expedition would have had to turn back. Henson came up with the solution to another vexing problem: the pemmican was frozen so hard that it cut their mouths, so he boiled it in the tea.

On the second day, they piled up again, separated from Bartlett's and Borup's parties by a lead. By the following morning, the sound of crunching ice told them the lead was closing. They made their way across and picked up Bartlett's trail. They saw by Borup's tracks that he had turned back according to plan to bring up more supplies from Cape Columbia. Peary sent Ross Marvin and his men to help Borup and to bring back replacements for the alcohol and petroleum cans that somehow had sprung leaks.

The warming weather—the temperature had gone up to $-9°F$.—worried Peary even more than the leaking cans, because it meant more, and possibly impassable, leads in the ice. A note soon reached him from Bartlett that told him just that— Bartlett was stuck up ahead at what seemed to him to be the Big Lead. They caught up with him and sat there, helpless. Two days passed, three, four. . . . There was no sign of Borup and Marvin, and the anxiety and waiting were making everyone tense. The Eskimos were getting restless. Two asked to go back, saying they were sick. Two more fell unconscious from the fumes of the alcohol stove and were revived by Peary and Bartlett. Five days passed, six . . . and still nothing happened. Then finally the lead closed sufficiently for them to cross. They left a message for Borup and Marvin and traveled on in a group, unable to spread out because of the numerous leads. They saw seven leads on one day's march, all one-half to one mile wide and barely covered with young ice. Peary agreed with Bartlett that this whole series of leads was the Big Lead of fearful memory, and later soundings proved them right. The next day an Eskimo on a light sledge came racing into camp with the welcome news that Borup and Marvin were also safely over the leads and on their way with the fuel. The relief was great, and the action speeded up.

Henson's team replaced Bartlett's as the pioneer division. Dr. Goodsell and his team of two Eskimos took twelve dogs and went back to Cape Columbia, passing Borup and Marvin on their way up. Each team would be sent back at various points determined by Peary to lighten the party until only Peary's remained to make the last dash for the Pole. MacMillan, suffering from a painfully frostbitten heel, soon followed Dr. Goodsell, leaving a deliriously happy Borup to take his place and go farther north than he had expected.

Borup's joy gave way temporarily as a lead opened in front of them, forcing the men to cross on large stepping-stones of ice. Borup's team slipped and fell into the water, and only his quick reflexes and great strength hauled them out in time, saving the dogs and 500 pounds of vital provisions on the sledge. Another time a lead opened up between Bartlett's snow igloo and Peary's, within a foot of where a team of dogs was staked out. As Bartlett's little island started floating off, he and his team jumped to safety to Peary's side, which in turn threatened to break off, leaving Henson's spot isolated. They chose the largest floe and everybody clustered on it, but the fear of the ice unexpectedly opening under them was ever present.

The next few marches were short, as leads and broken sledges slowed Henson down. Peary felt that Henson's pioneering capabilities had fallen short, so he gave the job to Ross Marvin. Henson, Borup, and Bartlett followed with pickaxes to improve the trail for their teams and the Peary team.

Bartlett, Borup, and Marvin took soundings whenever they found open water, and they checked latitudes on every other march, if the sun permitted, to see how far north they were. The method of taking latitudes was complicated, involving a sextant and an artificial horizon created with mercury poured into a trough set in a box packed flat into the snow. The reader, lying flat on the ice, moved his head and his sextant until he saw the sun reflected from two optical lenses onto the mercury. From this reflection, he determined the distance of the sun's center from its zenith, then added the declination of the sun for that day and hour, given in printed tables for every place on earth. Other tables were used to calculate refraction of the lenses. Obviously, readings differed slightly from person to person, so the mean, or middle set of values, was used for the record.

The process for taking latitudes was exceedingly hard on eyes already irritated by glare and cold. Measuring longitude to make sure they were going due north was, Peary felt, an added burden in equipment weight and time spent that they could do without. He knew they could keep a straight course by dead reckoning with a compass. Ordinary compasses in the high Arctic are not completely accurate because they do not point north; they point to the North Magnetic Pole, which moves around in the islands at the top of Canada (recently it was at latitude 77° north and longitude 120° west), and Peary's compass would have pointed south and a bit west. That's not much use to a man going to the North Pole unless he makes the southern end of the needle his north. This is essentially what Peary did, and he corrected the compass course at noontime, when the sun was due south. (A gyro-compass, which does not depend on magnetism to show north and south, was large and would not have responded well to a rough ride on a sledge or to the extreme cold.)

If the group inadvertently went northwest or northeast rather than dead north, they would lose precious time and put an added drain on sup-plies, but at 90° of latitude they would still be at the Pole, where east, west, north, and south converge. At the equator, lines of longitude are sixty miles apart, and as you go north or south, the distance between longitudes narrows but is still wide enough to make longitude readings essential for determin-ing where you are. But when you get to latitudes around 87° north or south, the lines of longitude are so close that they cannot be plotted accurately. If at that latitude the Peary party happened on the longitude for Outer Mongolia, it would only be a short walk to the longitude for New York or Green-land or France or wherever. So why bother? That was Peary's reasoning, and today's navigators agree with him. (A few years later Robert Falcon Scott in the Antarctic would lug cumbersome equip-ment for taking time-consuming, unnecessary lon-gitude readings, a factor that contributed to the death by starvation and exposure of all the expedi-tion members.) So the Peary group followed their noses, more or less. This procedure was not as sci-entific as some of Peary's detractors thought it should have been, but it had gotten Peary and Henson and the Eskimos around the Far North without any trouble for years.

Now it was time for a less-than-joyous Borup to turn back with three Eskimos and twenty dogs. Borup, very young and on his first expedition, achieved a farthest-north record that only Peary, Henson, Fridtjof Nansen, and the Italian explorer Umberto Cagni had reached before then. Peary sent him back with the warning that he not let the Eskimos get ahead of him, for in their eagerness to get back they might not come to his rescue if anything went wrong. Five marches later, when it was the more experienced Ross Marvin's turn to go back with two more Eskimos, Peary told him, "Watch out for the leads, my boy."

There is a sense almost of prophecy in these warnings, for Ross Marvin did not make it back.

Marvin's distraught Eskimo companions brought the news to the *Roosevelt* that Marvin had drowned in the Big Lead. He was too far ahead of them, they said, and when they got to the lead all they saw was Marvin's fur jacket. Or it may have been that he was too far behind. It has been suggested that the Eskimos shot Marvin because he was falling behind or because he made them angry for some reason. The Eskimos did kill if they hated or feared someone, but there is no reason to believe that these tried and trusted men who had been with the expedition for a long time would suddenly turn into murderers. That they would then go back to Cape Columbia and pretend to be upset about the death is even more unlikely. If they killed for a reason they saw as justified, their custom was to ignore the matter once it had been accomplished. And they certainly would not have been capable of faking the emotions they showed; they believed such pretense would bring evil spirits to haunt them. Nor

110

had they any reason to fear being punished even if they had murdered Marvin, for who would punish them? The worst Peary could do was withhold the guns and other things he had promised them. If they were afraid, all they had to do was take the sledges and go back to Etah or another village or even start their own village. The truth, though, may never be known. (This story is complicated by the fact that one of Marvin's Eskimo companions much later made a religious confession admitting to the murder. Unfortunately, the Eskimos often sought to please their confessors by making their confessions as lurid as possible without regard to truth, just as they politely said whatever they thought an outsider wanted to hear.)

What did Peary say when he turned Bartlett back at almost 88° north? Probably that he was sorry, for a terribly disappointed Bartlett had been hoping all along to be chosen over Matt Henson to accompany Peary to the Pole. But Peary had no question in his mind about bringing Henson. They made a good team. Henson had accompanied him on all but one of his excursions on the ice; he was the best sledge and dog handler, better even than most of the Eskimos; he was the most clever repairman of broken sledges or gadgets or whatever; he was more adept at speaking the Eskimo language than anyone else; and he was, Peary thought, safer with him because he felt Henson lacked the initiative and imagination to solve any problems on the way back. And Peary, ever the patriot, did not want to share the honor of reaching the Pole with a British subject (Bartlett was from Newfoundland) or with a young man who had not put years of his life into Arctic exploration, as he and Henson had.

Peary had also chosen the best Eskimos for the dash: Ootah and Egingwah, who had been with him on the previous expedition (Ootah was legendary among his own people for his sledging skills; Egingwah had been with Clark and had survived by eating his spare kamiks), Seegloo, and Ooqueah. They had the forty best dogs and the five best sledges. And they had 133 nautical miles to go.

Peary kept his exhilaration in check; he had long ago forbidden himself to imagine being successful, since all too often success had been plucked from his grasp. This time, however, he felt he was too close to fail. The men, the dogs, the sledges—all were in top condition. The six men had the vast experience needed to meet the challenges that nature might throw at them. "On, on we pushed," he wrote, "and I am not ashamed to confess that my pulse beat high, for the breath of success seemed already in my nostrils."

It was coming to the time of the full moon, which raised the tides that would open those dreaded leads. Peary was anxious to move fast and get back fast, before they might be cut off forever from the rest of the world. The thought that no one would ever know of his accomplishment horrified him more than the thought of death. But progress was slow as the north wind pushed the ice and the fragile men on the ice to the south, taking back some of their hard-won miles.

Five marches past the 88th parallel, Peary stumbled as he ran, and a sledge runner passed over his right foot. Then they faced a lead about 100 yards wide, covered with young ice. The men sent dogs and sledges ahead. The dogs crossed safely. Then it was the men's turn. Some got down on all fours and crawled; some glided on their snowshoes. The ice buckled beneath them. Peary later wrote that "A man who should wait for the ice to be really safe will stand small chance of getting far in these latitudes. . . . Often a man has the choice between the possibility of drowning by going on or starving to death by standing still, and challenges fate with the briefer and less painful choice."[3]

The next day a lead worked for instead of against them. Running north and south, covered by young ice thick enough to support the entire party, it became a highway to the Pole. They fairly flew over the smooth surface until the lead gave out. But traveling was still good, and their marches got longer. Their urgency was communicated to the dogs, and the air rang with the zinging of sledge runners and the bass fiddle *thump, thump, thump* of the men's feet pounding on the ice, faster and faster. . . .

Then, suddenly, it was over.

At 10:00 A.M. on April 6, 1909, they made camp. Peary named it Camp Morris K. Jesup. The latitude was 89°57" north. The Pole was theirs.

Henson took off his glove and offered his hand to Peary, who didn't see it, possibly because of his deep fatigue or the irritation in his eyes from taking the latitude reading. This incident received a lot of attention later on. Some said that Peary was ashamed to take Henson's hand because he really hadn't reached the Pole; others said that he was angry because Henson and the Eskimos really got there before he did—an impossibility. Whatever the reason, the incident would become much larger than either Henson or Peary could have imagined.

Finally, with snow igloos built and a meal eaten, Robert Edwin Peary could not keep his eyes open. At the moment of victory, he went to sleep. "The accumulated weariness of all those days and nights of forced marches and insufficient sleep, constant peril and anxiety, seemed to roll across me all at once," he wrote. "I could not sleep long. It was, therefore, only a few hours later when I woke. The first thing I did after awakening was to write these words in my diary: 'The Pole at last. The prize of three centuries. My dream and goal for two years. Mine at last! I cannot bring myself to realize it. It seems all so simple and commonplace!' "[4]

There was nothing there to distinguish the fabled Pole from any other place—no landmark, no sense of reaching a summit as a mountain climber would enjoy, nothing but more of the snow and ice they had traveled over for weeks. Neither was there a way to let anyone know that one of the world's great prizes had been won.

To confirm their achievement, Peary prepared to take another latitude reading at 6:00 P.M., but the sun was obscured. Instead, he and two of the men took a light sledge and went due north, finally stopping to take a reading when the sun cleared. The reading showed they had gone beyond the Pole. He later wrote, "It was hard to realize that, in the first miles of this brief march, we had been traveling due north, while on the last few miles of the same march, we had been traveling south, although we had all the time been traveling precisely in the same direction." They had sledged over the top of the world.

On their return to Camp Jesup, Peary took another series of observations, the highest 89° 58'37" north, indicating a position of four to five miles from the Pole. So he took a double team of dogs and a light sledge and traveled toward the sun and back. He went back and forth, quartering the area: "In traversing the ice in these various directions as I had done, I had allowed approximately ten miles for possible errors in my observations, and at some moment during these marches and countermarches, I had passed over or very near the point where north and south and east and west blend into one."⁵ More observations were made, all showing readings of virtually 90°, and then it seemed time for some sort of ceremony. Peary had brought with him Jo's guidon, tattered by years of being worn around his body on his various journeys and missing pieces that he had left at his various farthest-north cairns. Now he put a piece of the guidon in a glass bottle with two messages claiming the Pole for the United States and the Peary Expedition. The men set out the bottle and flags, and Henson led the Eskimos in a rousing three cheers. They did not understand the meaning of all this, but they entered into the spirit of things with great enthusiasm. Like any other travelers, Peary and Henson took photographs, and Peary wrote a postcard to Jo:

> 90 North Latitude, April 7th
>
> My dear Jo,
> I have won out at last. Have been here a day. I start for home and you in an hour. Love to the "kidsies."
>
> Bert.

Since no one could sleep, Peary decided to start the return journey. He impressed upon the men that it was essential to reach land before the next spring tides could further open the leads and before high winds shifted the ice and distorted the trail back. If they could stay on that trail, the ice would be already tamed, and the snow igloos they had built on the northward marches would be waiting for them.

They made two marches a day rather than one, cutting back on sleep. Their sledges were far lighter now than on the journey up, and the wind was at their backs, pushing them and the ice toward the south. Except for one day of gale, the weather was good, and there was no eastward movement of the ice at all. The lightness of the sledges allowed the party to cross young ice over leads that would not have borne the weight of fully loaded sledges. There were many leads to be crossed, but none delayed them more than two hours. And then, in the far distance, they saw the mountains of Grant Land. Only a few more days and they would be on land once again. But there was still the Big Lead to cross, the lead that had almost prevented the last expedition from ever getting back. Then they were finally there, and the Big Lead had disappeared—it was frozen over.

The sun was hot and searing, although temperatures ranged between − 18° and − 30°F. Bert's face was intolerably sore from sunburn. Did he think of the bonnet his mother had made him wear when he was a small child to protect his fair skin? How fair he must have been, if years of outdoor living had not toughened his skin sufficiently to prevent burning now. In addition to the sunburn, Peary suffered from the perspiration that dripped inside his fur clothing, coupled with the effects of quinine he had taken for a bad sore throat. But fortunately his leg no longer pained him. Then all his aches were forgotten when the glacial ice of Grant Land was under their feet and they were off the sea ice. The Eskimos shouted and danced with glee until they were exhausted. Ootah exclaimed, *"Tornarsuk . . .* is asleep or having trouble with his wife or we should never have come back so easily!"

On April 23 at 6:00 A.M. the group reached Cape Columbia, fifty-three days and forty-three marches after they had started out. The Eskimos built snow igloos, and the six men slept for the better part of two days. Then they went on to the *Roosevelt,* which was waiting patiently to gather the wanderers in.

VICTORY—AGONY

The victorious voyagers raced toward the *Roosevelt*. They saw Bob Bartlett clambering over the side of the still-listing ship to meet them, but they could see no joy on his face as they drew closer. Where were the others? After a brief greeting and words of congratulation, Bartlett told them of Ross Marvin's death.

Peary was devastated. He had never lost one of his men before, with the exception of Verhoeff, who was not really one of them and who had gone off on his own against Peary's orders. Now Peary felt grief and a sense of responsibility in addition to the natural depression that often follows the attainment of a long-desired end. Some people ease a sudden letdown like that by getting lots of sleep or by eating lots of food. Peary did both. "I had no energy or ambition for anything. Scarcely could I stop sleeping long enough to eat, or eating long enough to sleep."[1]

It would be a while before there was a celebration, and then Marvin's death threw a shadow over it. There was a feast, and Peary and his men presented the Eskimos with rifles, shotguns, cartridges, shells, reloading tools to make more ammunition, hatchets, knives, and highly valued telescopes that would allow them to spot game from afar.

While they waited for the *Roosevelt* to free itself from the ice, the men kept busy. They went after the unused caches that had been laid down in Greenland and Axel Heiberg Island in case any of the returning teams found themselves east or west of Cape Columbia when they got off the sea ice. Borup and the Eskimos built cairns to commemorate the expedition and to memorialize Ross Marvin. MacMillan took off for Fort Conger to make tidal observations, and Henson, Bartlett, and Peary cleaned the ship.

At the beginning of July, the ice loosened its grip on the *Roosevelt*. The ship slowly righted itself, and in four or five days it was once again on an even keel. The coal that had been stored on shore was returned to the ship, other chores were completed, and on July 18, the Peary Arctic Expedition started on the long voyage home.

Not far into that voyage, at stops at the villages of Nerke and Etah, Peary heard some distressing news: Dr. Frederick A. Cook was claiming that he had attained the Pole the year before. He had not announced it before, Cook said, because he was busy exploring Jones Sound at the south end of Ellesmere Island, and then he had gone to Upernavik, Greenland, to the south, in search of passage home. Failing to find a ship, Cook said, he made the long trip back to Etah. He arrived there without dogs, almost starved, only weeks before the Peary expedition. At Etah Cook argued with the two men Peary had stationed there. The men refused to give Cook his supplies until Harry Whitney persuaded them at gunpoint. Then Cook was given passage on a ship going to Denmark with the famous Danish-Eskimo explorer Knud Rasmussen, who believed Cook's claim to have achieved the Pole.

No one in the Peary party and none of the Eskimos believed that Cook had reached the Pole. Cook's sledges showed little sign of wear on the runners, an indication that they had not battled sea ice for any length of time. Nor were there enough sledges to have carried anywhere near the amount of supplies Cook and the Eskimos would have needed. Peary questioned the two Eskimos who had gone with Cook, and Borup and Dr. Goodsell recorded the answers in their diaries. The Eskimos said Cook was lying about making a long trip on the sea ice. They stated that he had been a poor traveler over the short length of sea ice they had been on and that they had never been out of sight of land. One of the Eskimos indicated by pointing to a map that they had gone to the top of Axel Heiberg Island, then south to Devon Island and Cape Sparbo.

Annoyed and angered, but unworried, Peary went about the usual business of bartering for furs and, he hoped, the scarce narwhal tusks. Also as usual, he saw to it that the Eskimos in each village he visited had sufficient meat for the winter; to provide it, he sent his men out to hunt. "We left them better supplied with the simple necessities of Arctic life than they had ever been before, while those who had participated in the sledge journey and the winter and spring work on the northern shore of Grant Land were really so enriched by our gifts that they assumed the importance of Arctic millionaires. . . .

It was not without keen regret that I looked my last upon these strange and faithful people who had meant so much to me."[2] Peary said good-bye to these people, without whom he could never have achieved his goal. Then he left the Arctic forever.

At this time Peary might have felt uneasy about the Cook affair, but he didn't show any sign of it. He hadn't a single doubt that the world would believe him when he said that Cook had lied. Today, when radio and television cameras and helicopters monitor every event, we see this as naïveté. But in Peary's time, the world accepted an explorer's word because there was nothing else to accept. (This is why some people adopted that habit of bringing a few natives back like zoo specimens to prove their claim.) There was nothing to bring back from the Pole. It never occurred to Peary that the world would think that *he* was lying, that it would cast him aside, that he would be forced to submit to examinations, indignities, and embarrassments. Never could he have imagined the bitterness that lay before him, for Cook's word was taken over his simply because Frederick Cook uttered it first.

The *Roosevelt* put in at Indian Harbor, Labrador, on September 5, and Peary's first telegram was to Jo: "Have made good at last. I have the Pole. Am Well. Love." After making Bartlett send a wire to his mother, Peary telegraphed Herbert L. Bridgman of the Peary Arctic Club the code message "Sun," meaning that he had reached the Pole and the *Roosevelt* was safe. He also telegraphed the news services: "Stars and Stripes nailed to the Pole." As they traveled down to Sydney, reporters came out on tugs to meet them. Jo and the children were waiting at Sydney, and the whole town turned out, with bands playing and bunting everywhere. Peary was exhilarated and looked forward to a glorious reception from his fellow Americans.

But there would be no reception, no welcome. Five days before Peary reached Indian Harbor, Cook had telegraphed from the Shetland Islands his story that *he* had attained the Pole the previous year. As Peary traveled home, Cook was being given a hero's welcome in Denmark after having been received by King Haakon VII the day after he had landed there.

Peary was a rational man and thought that the rational presentation of his case and the failure of Cook to present adequate proof of his claim would make people realize they had been taken in by a charlatan. He did not understand the impact of Cook's charisma on the public. He did not understand how the public could accept Cook's claim that he had told his Eskimo companions to lie about his attainment of the Pole so that no one would know he had reached the Pole until he was ready to announce it—he never explained what he had been waiting for. In fact, Cook hardly explained anything, remaining quiet and simply smiling gently. His reserved demeanor won him friends and supporters.

Peary, on the other hand, burned up the telegraph wires fighting and explaining, and the public thought he was a sore loser. He pointed out the flaws in Cook's claim, but that only aroused sympathy for Cook and resulted in a demand that he himself submit more adequate proofs. The same people who had accepted Cook without question turned on Peary with a barrage of offensive questions. Racists asked why had he not taken a white man with him. Why had he turned back the white men who could have verified his latitude readings? (Matt Henson could have taken the readings if Peary had wanted him to.) Why had he not taken longitude readings? Why did he go to sleep after he reached the Pole?

How dare he call such an obvious gentleman like Cook a liar? How dare he do . . . how dare he not do? Peary could do no right. Cook could do no wrong. Peary was stiff and arrogant in his manner, despising the need to defend himself, bewildered by the doubts, questions, and dislike surrounding him where once there had been nothing but admiration and success.

Men who hated Peary—including Greely, Sverdrup, Dedrick, and a few other expedition members whom Peary had alienated—fueled the fire. Friends—and he still had friends in high places—advised Peary to say nothing more; they believed that Cook's deceit would soon be uncovered. Peary, however, insisted he had to make his countrymen understand that Cook was lying to them, and so he continued to explain, demonstrate, and remonstrate. Meanwhile, Cook explained nothing. He simply responded benignly that he would be glad to "share" the honor of the discovery with Peary, since Peary seemed to need it so badly. This enraged Peary even more. The newspaper battle went back and forth, and Cook won it hands down. Then the laughter started, and the sarcastic jokes began. The public was tired of both men.

A small book entitled *The Cook-Ed Up Peary-Odd-Ical Dictionary* became something of a best-seller with entries like the following:

Artificial horizon—*A theoretical addition to the landscape at the theoretical Pole.*
Barter—*Arctic explorer's term for swapping a 12 cent knife for $300 worth of furs.*
Expedition party—*One that goes so far north no one can prove they didn't.*
Explore (v.)—*To loop glacial loops in search of a Pole that is not there.*

We were never quite certain before and so we used to ask, "What lies about the North Pole?" But we are no better off since the discoveries, for we are now asking, "Who lies about it?"

And so it went. Things got more serious among the scientists and the politicians. King Haakon VII of Denmark, worried that he might have been gulled, had the University of Copenhagen demand proof from Cook. Cook presented a sixty-one-page type-written report of his trip similar to the one he had written for a New York newspaper. This could have been fiction; it was not proof of anything except that Cook could write. Knud Rasmussen, who had originally championed Cook when he brought him to Denmark, was shocked and called the papers "a scandal . . . most impudent." When asked for his field notes, Cook said they were back in Etah among his supplies, which Peary's two men had not let him retrieve. But he *did* get his supplies, albeit at gun-point, so why would he have left such important material behind? After a very long delay, Cook supplied what he said were notes taken in the field, but no one could say for sure when they were actually written. Cook offered to have his Eskimos verify his discovery, but he never produced them.

Knud Rasmussen returned to Greenland and spoke with both Cook's and Peary's Eskimos. The son of an Eskimo mother and a Danish father, Rasmussen could question the Eskimos better than anyone else in the world. Egingwah and Ooqueah told Rasmussen of their journey in simple terms—exactly as Peary had reported it. Cook's Eskimo companions repeated that they had never been out of sight of land. Rasmussen, certain now that Cook had lied, repudiated him, as did the Danish government and other explorers and scientists.

Peary withheld his field notes from public view, fearful that Cook might use the information in some way. He paid for an examination of his records by the U.S. Coast and Geodetic Survey, just as corporations pay auditors to verify their records. Peary's accounts were found valid. Three men of impeccable credentials—Henry Gannett of the U.S. Geological Survey, Admiral Colby M. Chester of the U.S. Navy, and O. H. Tittmann of the Coast and Geodetic Survey—were appointed to a subcommittee of the National Geographic Society to investigate the Peary material, and they, too, found it valid.

The people of Europe recognized Peary's feat long before his fellow Americans did. In April 1910 the Peary family sailed to London and then traveled to Berlin, Rome, Vienna, Budapest, Saint Petersburg, Paris, Brussels, Antwerp, Dublin, and Edinburgh for the presentation of honorary degrees and medals to Robert E. Peary for his discovery of the North Pole.

Then, after his return to the United States, Peary stood before the House of Representatives in early January 1911. His friends had initiated a bill to promote him to rear admiral and retire him as of the date on which he had reached the North Pole almost two years before. It would mean official government acknowledgment of his accomplishment, and more—recognition of his veracity. The Senate had voted for the promotion, but there were men in the House whose ignorance of the Arctic was abysmal. One congressman addressing Peary epitomized their ignorance when he said, "I am advised by a school of scientists that it is a physical impossibility for man or beast to reach the North Pole for the reason that the diminishing centrifugal action . . . in proportion to the increasing center of gravity near the Pole, causes a complete failure of man and animal energy that produces a kind of paralysis of the senses and of motion, a paralysis of sensation in any part of the body, including the exercise of the faculty of the mind. . . . It would be almost impossible for them to exercise their independent functions so that anybody could ascertain a real fact—intelligently ascertain a fact."[3]

How could Peary answer such nonsense? His very presence gave lie to that theory, or gave lie to his own achievement of the Pole. But by now he had learned the value of silence, and it was a hard-learned lesson. He simply said he had never heard of such a thing. His interrogator was nonplussed. Never heard of it? Never. And he said no more.

This whole thing had its humorous side. Cook had even written to the congressional committee offering to step aside so that "Mr."—not "Commander"—Peary would receive "the honors—the retirement with increased pay." How kind of Cook to offer to step aside from a position he did not have, and to couch his offer in such charitable terms!

Finally, two months later, on March 3, 1911, Peary received the news that the bill had been made an act of Congress. He had been made a rear admiral and had been retired as of April 6, 1909, with "the thanks of the Congress."

He had won.

But it was too late for the trappings of victory. No one could give him back all he had suffered and lost in the two years since he had reached the Pole.

Life did settle down for the Pearys, who divided their year between their home in Washington, D.C., and the one Peary had designed and built on his beloved Eagle Island in Maine. Peary has sometimes been referred to as an exile at Eagle Island, a prisoner of public opinion. To the contrary, to him the island meant freedom. He loved its isolation, its natural beauty. He loved the woods and the sea breaking into waves against the rocks. He loved the birds and the animals. And Jo and the children loved having their husband and father at home—at last.

Peary also liked being in the center of things, and what better place for that than Washington, D.C.? They would spend the summer in Maine and go back to the capital in October or November. He was still the president of the American Geographical Society. (This had resulted in a sharp drop in enrollment, but that fact had been kept from him, for it would have been too much for him to bear.) He received requests to review books, write articles, and lecture. This, along with his voluminous correspondence, kept him busy.

Peary wrote a foreword to Matt Henson's book, *A Negro Explorer at the North Pole*, even though he had asked the expedition members not to publish books. The agreement was oral in Henson's case, since he alone had not signed a contract. Without Henson's knowledge, Peary gave the publisher $500 to publicize the book so it would have better sales. The book had some inconsistencies that played into the hands of some of Peary's old foes in the never-ending North Pole fight. For that matter, inconsistencies in Peary's own book about the Pole discovery had the same effect. Too busy to fulfill his book contract, Peary had allowed it to be ghostwritten, and small errors of fact had crept in.

But as far as Peary was concerned, the Arctic was a thing of the past. He had new interests. He championed the cause of that neglected invention, the "aeroplane." He had grasped its potential from the time of the Wright brothers' first flight at Kitty Hawk, North Carolina, in 1903. Amazingly, nothing much had happened in the next years to help the airplane achieve its potential. Peary was among the very first to try to make the government aware of the commercial and military importance of air power. When World War I erupted in Europe in 1914, Peary traveled widely to speak about the need for air power and a two-ocean navy for the United States. Peary knew better than most that moving ships through the Panama Canal between the oceans would take too much time in the event of war. He also foresaw the need for an air force separate from the Army and the Navy, a need the government did not recognize until the middle of World War II. He was chairman of an organization called the Aerial Coast Patrol, which would provide three hundred trained pilots for military duty when the United States entered the war in 1917.

But the Cook controversy was not yet dead. In 1916 a congressman from North Dakota sponsored a bill to repeal the act acknowledging Peary's achievement of the Pole. It began, "Whereas the various alleged Arctic discoveries claimed to have been made at certain times and on sundry expeditions by Civil Engineer Peary have been proven fictitious," and it called for Peary's demotion and the withdrawal of the thanks of Congress. The congressman had been persuaded to present the bill by a lobbyist hired by Dr. Cook, apparently with the assistance of Adolphus Greely, who was now a general.

Peary also retained the services of a lobbyist to help him through the legislative maze, as he had the first time. But this time around, Peary said nothing to defend himself to the outside world, and the matter simply died for lack of interest. Cook did not pay his lobbyist and wound up in a lawsuit.

A few years later Cook wound up in federal prison for mail fraud: after the North Pole fiasco he had taken to selling shares in fly-by-night companies promising great riches from oil lands in Texas.

Cook's defenders point out that oil was indeed found on some of these lands, but they neglect to say that it was many years later, long after the companies, along with the investors' money, had disappeared.

When America entered World War I, Peary volunteered for duty in whatever capacity the Navy could use him, but by this time his health was failing. Doctors diagnosed his condition as pernicious anemia, a chronic and incurable disease in which the red blood cells that carry essential oxygen from the lungs to every part of the body are not produced in sufficient numbers. Blood transfusions helped, and by the spring and summer of 1918, he seemed a lot better. In answering a fellow sufferer's letter of support, Bert wrote, "I have not at any time felt any apprehension in regard to my condition because I could not believe that a perfectly sound, smooth running machine could be put out of condition permanently because the steam pressure had run a bit low."[4]

Peary was wrong. The steam pressure ran lower and lower. In January 1919 he made his last public appearance, to honor Vilhjalmur Stefanson for his work in the Arctic. Appearing with him was General Adolphus Greely; the enmity between the two men had finally sputtered out.

Peary spent the summer of 1919 at Eagle Island, Maine, but there were no more brisk walks in the woods. The Pearys left for Washington earlier than usual so he could resume treatments, particularly blood transfusions. At the beginning of February, 1920 he had his thirty-fifth and final transfusion; the doctors at the naval hospital told him he had one week to live. Characteristically, Peary clung to life for almost a month. Then, on February 28, 1920, at 1:20 A.M. Robert Edwin Peary died.

Jo had this to say:

No one will ever know how the attack on my husband's veracity affected him, who had never had his word doubted in any thing at any time in his life. He could not believe it. And the personal grilling which he was obliged to undergo at the hands of Congress, while his scientific observations were examined and worked out, although it resulted in his complete vindication, hurt him more than all the hardships he endured in his sixteen years of research in the Arctic regions and did more toward the breaking down of his iron constitution than anything experienced in his explorations.[5]

EPILOGUE

Robert Peary's death did not end the controversy about his achievement of the North Pole. That controversy no longer focuses on Cook's claim. No one with serious knowledge gives credence to that, although a few writers haul Cook out of the closet every so often because "exposés" are lucrative, true or not. Unfortunately, no matter how unfair or wrong, some of the mud sticks in the readers' minds or gets passed on by writers who do not do their homework. One example is of an author who obviously did not want to spend time unraveling the Peary-Cook controversy for a book to which the material was only peripheral; he offered vague thumbnail sketches of the two men. Cook, he said, was gentle, charming, helpless against the establishment; Peary was autocratic, even frightening, and entrenched in the establishment. Then he told readers to make up their minds on that basis alone about which man had reached the Pole! Another writer had a hidden motive: he would be the first man to reach the North Pole on foot if Peary were to be discredited.

In January 1990 the *National Geographic* published a summary of the results of an investigation into the controversy by the Navigation Foundation of Baltimore, Maryland. Their year-long investigation included a complex analysis, called photogrammetric rectification, of Peary's and Henson's photographs and a minute examination of 225 cubic feet of Peary's papers at the National Archives and collections elsewhere, including the Peary-MacMillan Arctic Studies Center at Bowdoin College. Their conclusions were, briefly:

- Peary was correct in traveling by dead reckoning instead of wasting precious time on longitude readings, which that far north would have been "essentially useless."
- The distances recorded for the marches on the return journey were reasonable, not too fast as had been alleged. Other explorers and Peary himself had recorded as fast and even faster journeys.
- The soundings made by Marvin and Bartlett were subjected to scrutiny using a computer-generated model that showed them to be consistent with the expedition's recorded course.
- One critic had used records of ice movements to show that the expedition was west of the stated course. This critic was proved wrong by twenty miles. He had plotted a recorded shift of ice westward, but had neglected to figure in a subsequent entry about a heavy shift to the east that had put the expedition back on track.

- A contemporary writer had said one of Peary's lists was a secret record of compass variations showing he had really been off course and knew it. The Baltimore study showed that it was merely a list of serial numbers of Peary's chronometers.
- The expedition's latitude readings were essentially correct, as shown by photogrammetric analysis. The complicated process of analyzing photographs started with obtaining Peary's camera from the 1906 expedition. (Peary's farthest-north point for this expedition had also been disputed. Some said he had faked it to outdo the farthest-north record of Umberto Cagni, but the analysis of a photograph taken at noon at that latitude showed that Peary had indeed attained the record. He had, in fact, reached a slightly higher latitude than his reading showed.) The 1906 camera was adjusted to the focal length of Peary's 1909 camera, which could not be found and whose style had to be determined with the help of the Eastman Kodak Company. Shadows in the photograph were used to find the sun's elevation. The sun's elevation in respect to the placement of the camera lens was determined by a series of lines of perspective drawn by an artist; then latitudes were determined by mathematical computation. The average taken from five Peary photographs confirmed that Peary was at or very close to where he had said he was.
- The investigators concluded that Peary, Henson, Ootah, Egingwah, Seegloo, and Ooqueah had reached the North Pole.

The report ended, "In the light of all the data we have assimilated and analyzed, the board members of the Navigation Foundation have unanimously agreed that Peary realized his lifelong goal by attaining the North Pole on the last of his many expeditions. We found no evidence to the contrary. And, on a personal note, we cannot but hope that this marks the end of a long process of vilification of a courageous American explorer."

SOURCE NOTES

Prologue
1. The *Congressional Record,* U.S. Government Printing Office, Washington, D.C., publishes transcripts of the daily proceedings of both houses of Congress.

Chapter I
1. Letters to mother dated February 28 and March 7, 1868. The early Peary diaries, letters, and other papers have not been published except in secondary sources. These and the following excerpts, unless otherwise noted, are from *Peary: The Explorer and the Man* by John Edward Weems, who had access to the originals through the courtesy of the Peary family.
2. Peary diary of 1873.
3. Letter to Mary Kilby dated October 10, 1877.

Chapter II
1. Letter to mother dated February 3, 1881.
2. Letter to mother, August 16, 1880.
3. Unaddressed note written in 1881.
4. Letter to mother completed December 28, 1884.
5. Peary diary entries of 1885.
6. Weems, John Edward, *Peary: The Explorer and the Man,* p. 89.

Chapter III
1. Letter from Peary to mother, June 11, 1891.
2. Peary, Josephine Diebitsch, *My Arctic Journal,* p. 85.
3. *Ibid.,* p. 90.
4. *Ibid.,* p. 122.
5. *Ibid.,* p. 287.

6. Peary, Robert E., *Northward over the Great Ice,* vol. 1, p. 210.

Chapter IV
1. Peary, Josephine D., *The Snow Baby,* p. 12.
2. Peary, Robert E., *Northward over the Great Ice,* vol. 2, p. 111.
3. Preston, Douglas J., *Dinosaurs in the Attic: An Excursion into the American Museum of Natural History,* p. 51.
4. Weems, John Edward, *Peary: The Explorer and the Man,* pp. 155–157.

Chapter V
1. Peary, Robert E., *The North Pole,* p. 94.
2. Weems, John Edward, *Peary: The Explorer and the Man,* p. 181, from a speech made by Peary at Rensselaer Polytechnic Institute, Troy, New York.
3. Letter from Peary to wife dated August 27, 1899.
4. Letter from Josephine Peary to husband, dated August 28, 1900.
5. Peary diary entry November 1900.
6. Letter dated April 4, 1901.

Chapter VI
1. Peary, Robert E., *Nearest the Pole,* pp. 146–147.
2. *Ibid.,* pp. 168–169.

Chapter VII
1. Peary letter to Herbert Bridgman of the Peary Arctic Club dated April 12, 1908.
2. Peary, Robert E., *The North Pole,* pp. 198–199.
3. *Ibid.,* p. 281.
4. *Ibid.,* p. 288.
5. *Ibid.,* p. 291.

Chapter VIII
1. Peary, Robert E., *The North Pole,* p. 323.
2. *Ibid.,* pp. 333–334.
3. Weems, John Edward, *Peary: The Explorer and the Man,* pp. 290–292.
4. Letter from Peary to Rev. Thornton F. Turner of New York City, dated May 27, 1918.
5. From an undated note.

BIBLIOGRAPHY

Anderson, Madelyn K. *Greenland: Island at the Top of the World.* New York: Dodd, Mead, 1983.

Anonymous. *The Cook-Ed-Up Peary-Odd-Ical Dictionary and Who's Hoot.* Boston: Luce, 1910.

Bartlett, Robert A. *The Log of Bob Bartlett.* New York: Putnam, 1928.

Berton, Pierre. *The Arctic Grail: The Quest for the North West Passage and the North Pole, 1818–1909.* New York: Viking, 1988.

Borup, George. *A Tenderfoot with Peary.* New York: Stokes, 1911.

Cook, Frederick A. *My Attainment of the Pole.* New York: Mitchell Kennerey, 1912.

Davies, Thomas D. "New Evidence Places Peary at the Pole." *National Geographic,* vol. 177(1), January 1990, pp. 44–61.

———. *Robert E. Peary at the North Pole.* Rockville, Maryland: Foundation for the Promotion of the Art of Navigation, 1989.

Dyson, James L. *The World of Ice.* New York: Knopf, 1972.

Dyson, John. *The Hot Arctic.* Boston: Little, Brown, 1979.

Henson, Matthew A. *A Negro Explorer at the North Pole.* New York: Stokes, 1912. Reprint: *A Black Explorer at the North Pole.* Lincoln: University of Nebraska Press, 1989.

Herbert, Wally. *The Noose of Laurels: Robert E. Peary and the Race to the North Pole.* New York: Macmillan, 1989.

Hobbs, William Herbert. *The North Pole of the Winds.* New York: Putnam, 1930.

———. *Peary.* Macmillan, 1936.

Kent, Zachary. *The Story of Admiral Peary at the North Pole.* Chicago: Childrens Press, 1988.

Lopez, Barry H. *Arctic Dreams.* New York: Scribner's, 1986.

MacMillan, Donald B. *How Peary Reached the Pole.* Boston: Houghton Mifflin, 1934.

Malaurie, Jean. *The Last Kings of Thule.* New York: Dutton, 1982.

Morris, Charles, ed. *Finding the North Pole by Cook and Peary.* W. E. Scull, 1909.

Peary, Josephine Diebitsch. *My Arctic Journal.* New York: Contemporary, 1893.

———. *The Snow Baby.* New York: Stokes, 1901.

Peary, Robert E. *Nearest the Pole.* New York: Doubleday, 1907.

———. *The North Pole.* New York: Stokes, 1910. Reprint: New York: Dover, 1986.

———. *Northward over the Great Ice.* New York: Stokes, 1898.

Preston, Douglas J. *Dinosaurs in the Attic: An Excursion into the American Museum of Natural History.* New York: Random House, 1986.

Stafford, Marie Ahnighito Peary. *Discoverer of the North Pole.* New York: Morrow, 1959.

Walsh, Henry C. *The Last Cruise of the Miranda.* New York: Transatlantic, 1895.

Weems, John Edward. *Peary: The Explorer and the Man.* Boston: Houghton Mifflin, 1967.

INDEX

Ahngoodloo, 76, 78
Ahnighito, 59–61, 66
Airplanes, 126–27
Allakasingwah, 76–77,
  79–80
American Geographical So-
  ciety, 39, 67, 72, 85, 126
American Museum of Natu-
  ral History, 66, 72
Anniversary Lodge, 55–56,
  63
Astrup, Elvind, 41, 48–49,
  54, 55, 57, 62

Baldwin, Evelyn Briggs,
  54, 57, 58
Bartlett, Robert A., 87, 96,
  100, 105, 106–8, 111,
  117, 118, 120, 132
Big Lead, 89, 90–92, 97,
  106–7, 110, 116
Bill, Miss, 59, 61
Borup, George, 96, 102,
  105–8, 110, 118, 119
Bowdoin College, 19–21, 23,
  24, 132
Brainard, D. W., 78
Bridgman, Herbert L., 76,
  77, 79, 120
Brooklyn Institute, 39

Brooklyn Navy Yard, 37,
  66
Burton, Al, 24

Cagni, Umberto, 110, 133
Camp Morris K. Jesup,
  113–14
Cape Columbia, 102, 104,
  106, 107, 116, 118
Cape Morris K. Jesup,
  78–79
Cape Sabine, 79–80, 82
Cape Sheridan, 87–88, 93,
  100, 101–2
Cape Thomas Hubbard, 92
Cape Washington, 78
Carr, George H., 54, 55
Chester, Colby M., 124
Clark, Charles, 92, 112
Clark, George F., 54, 57, 58
Clothing, 40, 46
Compasses, 108–9
Congress, U.S., 11, 124–25,
  127, 128
Continental shelf, 89
Cook, Frederick A., 41, 42,
  45, 48, 49, 54, 97–99,
  118–25, 127–28, 131–32
*Cook-Ed Up Peary-Odd-Ical
Dictionary, The,* 122–23

Crane, Zenas, 96
Crocker Land, 92–93
Cross, Susan J., 54, 56, 59

Davidson, James, 54, 58
Dedrick, T. S., Jr., 73–76,
  81, 82, 84, 122
Diebitsch, Emil, 35, 61, 66

Eagle Island, 25–26, 125–
  26, 128
Egingwah, 10, 111–12,
  123, 133
Ellesmere Island, 30, 73,
  99, 118
Entrikin, Samuel J., 54, 58,
  61
Erik, 83, 84, 87, 97, 99
Eskimos, 9–10, 38, 41, 44,
  45, 55, 56, 58, 62–63, 72,
  73, 78, 84, 87, 90–91, 92,
  97, 99, 103, 105–7
  brought home by ex-
    plorers, 66–67
  clothing of, 46
  Cook and, 119, 121,
    123
  customs of, followed by
    Peary, 31, 40
  diet of, 88, 104
  fears of, 49–50, 64
  "iron mountain" and,
    59–61
  Marvin's death and,
    110–11
  Peary accompanied to
    North Pole by, 10,
    111–13, 115–16, 123,
    133
  Peary's provisions for,
    51, 118, 119–20
Eskimo women, 31, 46–47,
  58, 102
  expedition members'

relations with, 76–77,
  79–80, 81
Etah, 87, 97–98, 111, 118–
  19, 123

Falcon, 61
Fort Conger, 73–82, 87,
  118
Franke, Rudolph, 97–98, 99
Franklin, Sir John, 30

Gannett, Henry, 124
Gibson, Langdon, 41, 48,
  49–50
Goodsell, J. W., 96, 105,
  107, 119
Grant Land, 92, 93, 96,
  116
Greely, Adolphus, 30, 73,
  74, 75, 76, 78, 93, 122,
  127, 128
Greenland:
  established as island,
    64, 79
  Peary's first expedition
    to (1886), 32–34
  Peary's second expedi-
    tion to (1893–1895),
    53–67
  weather of, 64–65

Haakon VII, King of Den-
  mark, 121, 123
Heiberg, Axel, 92
Henson, Matt, 53–54, 77,
  109–10, 126, 132
  in expedition of 1891–
    1892, 41, 44, 45, 48,
    49–50
  in expedition of 1893–
    1895, 54, 58, 61–65
  in expedition of 1898–
    1902, 73–76, 78–79,
    81–82, 84

in expedition of 1905–
1906, 87, 90
in expedition of 1908–
1909, 96, 97, 100,
105, 107–8, 111–13,
115–16, 118, 121
Peary accompanied to
Pole by, 10, 111–13,
115–16, 133
Peary's relationship
with, 35, 65–66, 81–2
Hope, 72, 73
Hubbard, Thomas H., 96

Igloos, 40
Independence Bay, 48–49,
56–57, 63
International Polar Year
(1882), 30

Jesup, Morris K., 71–72,
76, 78, 86, 95
Jesup, Mrs. Morris K.,
95–96

Kane, Elisha Kent, 15–16,
30
Key West, Fla., 28–29
Kilby, Mary ("Mae"), 21,
24, 25
Kite, 39, 41–42, 43, 45, 66

Latitude readings, 108–10,
114–15, 121, 132
League Island Navy Yard,
38
Lee, Hugh J., 54, 57, 59–65
Lockwood, J. B., 78
Longitude readings, 108–
10, 121, 132

McKinley, William, 71
Macmillan, Donald B., 67,
92, 96, 102, 105, 107, 118

Maigaard, Christian, 33–34,
39, 44
Marvin, G., Ross, 87, 93,
96, 100–102, 105–8, 110–
11, 117, 118
Menocal, A. G., 28, 29, 35
Meteorites, 59–61, 66
Mirages, 92–93
Moore, Charles A., 71
Mylius-Erichsen, Ludvig,
49

Nansen, Fridtjof, 38, 101,
110
National Geographic,
132–34
National Geographic Soci-
ety, 124
Naval Academy, U.S., 28
Navigation Foundation,
132–34
Navy, U.S., 27–30, 34, 37,
38, 85, 96, 124, 127, 128
Panama Canal and, 29–
30, 35
Peary's leaves from, 41,
53, 71, 72, 86
*Negro Explorer at the
North Pole, A*, 126
New York Herald, 35, 36
New York Times, 36
Nicaragua, 25, 27–28, 29–
30, 34–36
Nordenskjöld, Baron Nils
Adolf Erik, 30, 34
Northcliffe, Lord, 72
Northeast Passage, 30
North Magnetic Pole, 108–
109
North Pole:
identification of, 69–71,
108–10, 114–15, 121,
132
Peary's first expedition

141

North Pole (*cont.*)
  to (1898–1902),
  69–84
Peary's second expedi-
  tion to (1905–1906),
  86–93
Peary's third expedition
  to (1908–1909), 95–
  120
reached by Peary, 10,
  111–15
Northwest Passage, 30, 59

Ooqueah, 10, 112, 123, 133
Ootah, 10, 111–12, 116,
  133

Panama Canal, 25, 27–28,
  29–30, 34–36, 127
Peary, Charles Nutter,
  13–14
Peary, Francine, 76
Peary, Josephine Diebitsch,
  37–38, 61–63, 73, 75, 77,
  87, 90, 96, 115, 120, 126,
  128–29
  in Arctic expedition of
    1891–1892, 40–51
  childbearing of, 53, 56,
    76, 85
  courtship and wedding
    of, 27, 30, 36, 37
  Eskimo women and,
    46–47, 79–80
  in expedition of 1893–
    1895, 53, 54, 56, 58–
    59, 61
  Peary Relief Expedition
    and, 66, 72
  surprise reunion and,
    79–80, 82–84
Peary, Marie Ahnighito, 56,
  59, 61, 63, 66, 79, 80, 82,
  83–84, 96, 120, 126

Peary, Mary Wiley, 13–17,
  19, 23, 25, 26, 29, 32, 34,
  38, 41, 58, 73, 83, 116
Peary, Robert E.:
  childhood of, 13–19
  as civil engineer, 20–
    21, 23–30, 34–36, 85
  courtship and wedding
    of, 27, 30, 36, 37
  death of, 128–29, 131
  education of, 16–21
  expedition tactics of,
    30–32, 39–41
  frostbitten toes of, 75–
    76, 79, 80, 85–86
  funding for expeditions
    of, 38–39, 53–54, 66,
    71–72, 86, 95–96
  leg broken by, 42, 43,
    45, 105
  life of, after Arctic ex-
    peditions, 125–28
  naval appointment of,
    27
  promoted to rear admi-
    ral, 11, 124–25
  as public speaker,
    53–55
  romances of, 18–19, 21,
    24, 25, 27, 36
  siren call of Arctic first
    heard by, 15–16
Peary, Robert E., Jr., 85,
  96, 100, 120, 126
Peary Arctic Club, 72, 76,
  86, 95, 96, 99, 120
Peary Land, 48, 92
Peary Relief Expedition, 66,
  72
Peary Route, 69, 72, 73
Percy, Charles, 83, 87, 88,
  100, 102
Permafrost, 43–44
Philadelphia Academy of

142

Natural Sciences, 39, 41, 42, 53
Portland High School, 17, 18, 19
Portland Museum of Natural History, 18

Rasmussen, Knud, 119, 123
Redcliffe, 44, 49
Roosevelt, 87–88, 90, 92, 93, 95, 96, 97, 100–103, 110, 116–18, 120
Roosevelt, Theodore, 86, 96
Ross, Sir John, 59, 92–93
Royal Geographic Society, 67
Royal Scottish Geographical Society, 85

Scott, Robert Falcon, 109
Seegloo, 10, 112, 133
Sharp, D. R., 42
Snow Baby dolls, 56
Société de Géographie, 85
Spanish-American War, 71, 72

Stefanson, Vilhjalmur, 128
Stokes, Frederick, 54
Storm Camp, 89
Sverdrup, Otto, 72, 73, 122
Swain, Wallace F., 54

Tallakoteah, 59–60
Tittmann, O. H., 124

Uisakavsak, 67
U.S. Coast and Geodetic Survey, 24–25, 27, 96, 102, 124

Verhoeff, John, 41, 50–51, 54, 55, 117
Vincent, Edwin E., 54, 58
Vose, George Leonard, 20

Whitney, Harry, 97, 119
Windward, 72, 73, 76, 79, 82, 83–84, 87
Wistar, Mount, 64, 79
Wolf, Louis G., 87
World War I, 127, 128
World War II, 65, 127
Wright brothers, 126

143

ABOUT THE
AUTHOR

Madelyn Klein Anderson traveled over the Arctic ice pack and the Greenland ice cap—in the comfort of the cockpit of a Coast Guard International Ice Patrol C130—and had her nose painted bright blue in honor of her first crossing of the Arctic Circle. The result was a permanent state of enchantment with the Arctic and a number of books. Mrs. Anderson is a former Army officer and editor of children's books who holds two graduate degrees, one in occupational therapy from New York University and the other in library science from Pratt Institute in Brooklyn, New York. She is currently a consultant with the New York City Public Schools and is writing several more books for Franklin Watts.